# Praise for *Instructional Leadership*

Peter DeWitt's book is clearly written from the heart, based on his own research and his extensive experience (and challenges faced) in many leadership roles. It is a book that will resound with, and be of immense value to, all existing and aspiring school leaders who attempt to balance the complexity of tasks and the demands of accountability and compliance, while also attempting to be leaders of learners.

—Kenneth Muir, Chief Executive and Registrar
General Teaching Council for Scotland

So much has been written on the topic of instructional leadership, but too little is known about how to implement it. DeWitt once again finds a balance between research and practice by focusing on implementation, developing program logics, and evidence of impact. He is offering a road map to help leaders put their focus on learning and build credibility with staff while doing it.

—John Hattie, Author, *Visible Learning*, and
Director of the Melbourne Education Research Institute,
University of Melbourne, Australia

The practical tips and reflections are highly informative. Continually DeWitt brings us back to the perception-reality gap that makes the day-to-day processes of educational leadership far more reactive than we think. As the author explains, what we *think* we do as educational leaders is often neither what our colleagues observe nor how time stacks up.

By following this practical recipe for instructional leadership, busy leaders can adjust their current practices to focus on that which matters most: improving the life chances of learners through increased impact in learning. Leadership will never be easy in an increasingly complex world, but the clarity with which this books unpacks the key ingredients will certainly make it easier.

—Steven Cox, Owner, Osiris Educational

*Instructional Leadership* is the nexus between the key instructional leadership research and the practical day-to-day role of the school leader. For the first time, here is a book that addresses and provides the "why" and "how" underpinned by an implementation framework that can successfully be adopted to support the learning of all school stakeholders when addressing any school improvement. The book identifies and provides clear examples for leaders on "what" instructional leadership, based on research and practice, can look like on a day-to-day basis that is effective for all leaders—from the classroom to district or regional roles. This should be a book read by all aspiring leaders; and by experienced leaders as a reflection of our current leadership and in response to the key questions DeWitt asks in each chapter. As he says in the beginning of the book, "This book is about defining a common language and common understanding" about instructional leadership. He has achieved what he set out to address.

—Helen Butler, Educational Leader, Melbourne, Australia

Principals have the potential to magnify and multiple effective instruction. But far too often, this potential is not realized. Peter DeWitt provides a pathway to get the job done. This thoughtful and practical guide will help you become the instructional leader you have always wanted to be. And, if you take his advice seriously, the students in your school will learn more and learn better. I promise.

—Douglas Fisher Author, Consultant, Professor
San Diego State University San Diego, CA

This book is long overdue! It is time instructional leaders heed the tools in this book to begin walking the walk of true instructional leaders. DeWitt clarifies that common language does not always equate to common understanding—it requires purposeful planning and design. He does a masterful job of defining instructional leadership and applying it through relatable situations throughout the book. This book alone would help to prevent what I refer to as SOS, Shiny Object Syndrome, in education. We have tended to consistently react to the newest and shiniest program or promise in education, and this has led to initiative overload and reactive leadership as opposed to proactive leadership and creating evidence of impact. The program logic model DeWitt demonstrates is a great way for leadership teams to create evidence of impact through dialogue and action and allow instructional leaders to shift their focus to how learning works and the concepts of learning.

—Todd Wiedemann, Co-Director, Kansas MTSS and Alignment

This book will help leaders to overcome the challenge of operationalizing instructional leadership. The six areas identified by DeWitt provide a clear and practical route map for developing the practice of instructional leadership. The mindful moments are timely and effective punctuations that help you to stop and think, process, and apply the learning. Likewise, the student voice questions ensure that we calibrate what we think with what our students say, do, and experience. As we move into an age with even greater focus on implementation and the fidelity of implementation, DeWitt's work will support leaders in developing and delivering clarity and action that will improve the life chance of our children and young people.

—Sarah Philp, Director of Learning Scotland
Osiris Educational, Edinburgh

Peter DeWitt tackles the topic of instructional leadership head-on as a researcher, consultant, coach and former school administrator. As is his style, he shares his findings as if the reader were having a personal conversation with him about the hard work of being an instructional leader and at the same time managing the day-to-day operation of the building. This work provides administrators with a road map in understanding this complex topic but, more importantly, identifies six areas of implementation. DeWitt provides a complete workshop wrapped up within the pages of this book. It is a must-read for school administrators who seek to understand how to implement improvements effectively, build collective efficacy and focus on student learning.

—Jim Verlengia, Adjunct Instructor,
Leadership School of Education, Drake University, Des Moines, IA

Peter DeWitt draws on research and personal experience as he skillfully unpacks the complexities involved in the practice of instructional leadership. School leaders will find the ideas in this book relatable, practical, and significant in relation to improving student outcomes. If you aspire to lead school improvement by strengthening the quality of classroom instruction and reaching deep levels of implementation, this book will provide the guidance you seek.

—Jenni Donohoo, PhD, Author and School
Improvement Consultant

Peter DeWitt has been a learner from day one since he first became a teacher, and especially shortly thereafter when he became a principal. In 2006 he enjoyed being a leader in a small rural community. Then he had a growing and compelling realization that something was wrong, and became what I would call a "positive rebel," devoting himself to making a difference. Now we have a short, focused book on what he has been learning over the past decade. "Instructional leadership" is a crystal-clear treatise on "mindful moments" organized around six principles. If you want to know what instructional leadership is—and, equally importantly, what it is not—this is the book for you. Clear models, guiding questions and insights, and a to-do list will have you leaning toward action from page 1. Read it, use it, and tell your friends.

—Michael Fullan, OC, Professor Emeritus
OISE/University of Toronto

Instructional leadership is something that we strive to foster in ourselves as well as those around us because we know, as leaders, it is the type of leadership that leads to the most significant impact on student success. This is not an easy task, as many of us do not fully understand what it means to be an instructional leader or how to successfully grow in that area. In this book, highly acclaimed author and consultant Peter DeWitt guides readers down the path to understanding and becoming an instructional leader through ideas that are grounded in research and presented with the aid of outstanding practical examples and models. If you are ready to begin your journey toward instructional leadership, this book is an excellent place to start!

—Heath Peine, Executive Director of Student Support Services
Wichita Public Schools

DeWitt brings the heart of a true leader to every sentence in this book. He illuminates important leadership concepts about instruction, social-emotional learning, and collective efficacy with a humanity that allows us to see the potential we hold.

DeWitt matches the courage to lead with the tools to do so and, in the process, lets readers see how coherence and clarity drive the growth of students and adults.

—Nancy Frey, Author, Consultant,
Professor San Diego State University, San Diego, CA

Blending personal experience, research, and observations acquired through coaching others, DeWitt offers important insights and practical guidance to school leaders aspiring to improve their students' life chances.

—Kenneth Leithwood, Educational Researcher and Professor,
Ontario Institute for Studies in Education,
Toronto, Canada

DeWitt's *Instructional Leadership: Creating Practice Out of Theory* provides practical solutions to the challenges of being an instructional leader within an educational system not designed to meet the needs of all students. It provides a clear and concise program logic model that I will be using to broaden the impact of our initiatives. This book inspires us and gives us tools to engage teachers and students to co-create inclusive and supportive learning environments that will support our efforts to achieve equity in our schools.

—Blanca Baltazar-Sabbah, Associate Superintendent,
Instructional Services, Salinas Union High School District

*Instructional Leadership* provides actionable research-based methods to help teams move the needle as instructional leaders in a concrete way. It feels as though Peter is coaching you through the process as you learn to utilize the tools provided to make your schools successful. A perfect choice for principals, assistant superintendents, and superintendents!

—Mary Ann Bryan, Assistant Superintendent
Instructional Services and Support, Weymouth Public Schools

Peter DeWitt's conversational writing style will engage all leaders. He is knowledgeable and confident in writing about leadership, as he has been there, done the work successfully, and now writes about "living in" the instructional leadership role. DeWitt challenges us to be reflective about the strategies that we collaboratively discern make a difference to attain *all* students' growth and achievement. His thinking is clear about what leaders must do to move *all* students forward. Most importantly DeWitt gives us the tools, like his comprehensive logic model, pithy myth-busters, real-life vignettes, reflective questions and mindful moments, to do the work together. This inspirational book is a must-read for all aspiring and seasoned leaders. DeWitt convinces us that leadership that makes a difference is doable, personalizing his content with narrative from his own lived experiences as a leader.

—Lyn Sharratt, Internship Supervisor
Ontario Institute for Studies in Education, University of Toronto, Canada
International Consultant, Author and Practitioner

This book is well-timed in a world where school leaders are expected to be instructional leaders but also building managers. Peter DeWitt understands that being an instructional leader is complicated, and this book has both challenged and reinforced my thinking around my leadership practices. His experience as a principal allows him to identify the many challenges and the important impact of instructional leadership on student achievement. He recognizes that, due to our competing responsibilities as leaders, we cannot be expected to focus solely on instructional leadership, yet we can set aside some time to focus on it. As leaders, we decide how much and when, but we need to commit to it to make it a part of our leadership time. This book helps identify the key components we need as leaders, as well as structures that will help us make a positive impact. It is a fantastic read if you are looking to find ways to balance the competing challenges of a leadership position. Thank you, Peter, for inspiring my instructional leadership as I begin my 17th year as a principal.

—Dave Westaway, Principal, TVDSB
Vice President of Ontario Principals' Council

Peter DeWitt sets out to connect research and practice—and he has succeeded! The two are interwoven superbly, resulting in a book that is both practical and wise. The chapters dig deeper into the meaning and practices of instructional leadership in ways that are relevant to an international readership.

—Elaine Munthe
Dean of the Faculty of Educational Sciences and the Humanities
University of Stavanger, Stavanger, Norway

# Instructional
# LEADERSHIP

*To Doug*
*Thank you for all of your support.*

*To family and friends*
*You always inspire me to be a better person.*

# Instructional
# LEADERSHIP

Creating
Practice
Out of
Theory

PETER M. DeWITT

CORWIN

A SAGE Publishing Company

For Information:

Corwin

A SAGE Company

2455 Teller Road

Thousand Oaks, California 91320

(800) 233-9936

www.corwin.com

SAGE Publications Ltd.

1 Oliver's Yard

55 City Road

London EC1Y 1SP

United Kingdom

SAGE Publications India Pvt. Ltd.

B 1/I 1 Mohan Cooperative Industrial Area

Mathura Road, New Delhi 110 044

India

SAGE Publications Asia-Pacific Pte. Ltd.

18 Cross Street #10-10/11/12

China Square Central

Singapore 049483

Publisher: Arnis Burvikovs

Acquisitions Editor: Ariel Curry

Development Editor: Desirée A. Bartlett

Senior Editorial Assistant:
  Eliza B. Erickson

Production Editor: Amy Schroller

Copy Editor: William DeRooy

Typesetter: Hurix Digital

Proofreader: Lawrence W. Baker

Indexer: Molly Hall

Cover Designer: Gail Buschman

Marketing Manager: Sharon Pendergast

Printed in the United States of America

*Library of Congress Cataloging-in-Publication Data*

Names: DeWitt, Peter M., author.

Title: Instructional leadership : creating practice out of theory / Peter M. DeWitt.

Description: First edition. | Thousand Oaks, California : Corwin, 2020. | Includes bibliographical references.

Identifiers: LCCN 2019046097 | ISBN 9781544381411 (paperback) | ISBN 9781544381435 (epub) | ISBN 9781544381442 (epub) | ISBN 9781544381428 (ebook)

Subjects: LCSH: Educational leadership. | School management and organization. | Communication in education.

Classification: LCC LB2806 .D485 2020 | DDC 371.2—dc23

LC record available at https://lccn.loc.gov/2019046097

This book is printed on acid-free paper.

20 21 22 23 24 10 9 8 7 6 5 4 3 2 1

# Contents

# About the Companion Website

This book's companion website features video content as well as printable resources and tools created to help leaders organize their thoughts around the most important components of instructional leadership. Included are the author's video introduction to each chapter, a template for the Program Logic Model, all of the Program Logic Model examples from this book, and several graphic organizers not present in the book. (See a description of each online resource on the pages that follow.)

Visit the companion website at
**resources.corwin.com/instructionalleadership**
or scan this QR code for the resources.

**Note From the Publisher:** The author has provided content that is available to you through QR codes. To read a QR code, you must have a smartphone or tablet with a camera. We recommend that you download a QR code reader app that is made specifically for your phone or tablet brand.

## ONLINE RESOURCES

**Peter DeWitt Introduces Each Chapter**

**Video 1.1 Instructional Leadership as a Holistic Approach**

**Video 2.1 The Logic Behind Implementation**

**Video 3.1 A Focus on Learning**

**Video 4.1 Student Engagement**

**Video 5.1 Instructional Strategies**

**Video 6.1 Collective Efficacy**

**Video 7.1 Evidence of Impact**

## Resource 1: Program Logic Model Template

Use this graphic organizer to create your own program logic model as a practice example, or use this with a group to begin focusing on your greatest area of need.

## Resource 2: Program Logic Model Examples

The book offers many examples of using a program logic model to implement specific initiatives. You can find a downloadable copy of each example here.

## Resource 3: Implementation Strategy for Instructional Leaders

The implementation strategy is an extension of the program logic model. Through this process of implementation, teachers and leaders can come together collectively, or leaders can work within their administrative team, to prepare for conversations with teachers and students. All of these groups learn from one another during the reflection/feedback process, which should ultimately have a positive impact on student learning.

## Resource 4: Knowledge Dimensions Graphic Organizer

Use this graphic organizer for an individual activity or a group activity. In the middle please jot down the collective thoughts you or the group learned from the chapter on knowledge dimensions. On the outside, write down examples of questions that would be considered factual knowledge, procedural knowledge, conceptual knowledge and metacognitive knowledge.

## Resource 5: Student Engagement Graphic Organizer

Use this graphic organizer to write your own definition of student engagement. Perhaps the definition you choose to write can be adopted as a common language and common understanding. In the three boxes below the definition, please write three ways that your staff engage students.

## Resource 6: Instructional Strategies Graphic Organizer

Please begin this organizer by explaining how staff in your school focuses on instructional strategies. Do they share best practices or model instructional strategies at faculty meetings, PLCs or in department meetings?

Throughout the chapter I offered methods of implementing strategies and gave deeper explanations of each. In the second row of this graphic organizer, write down three new pieces of information you learned about instructional strategies.

The third section of this graphic organizer stretches the thinking a bit. It is meant to help you move from three ideas you learned in the chapter on instructional strategies to inspiring you to find two instructional strategies you believe staff would like to try (whole staff or a small group of staff members).

## Resource 7: Evidence Collection Graphic Organizer

Using the same graphic organizer that was created to help your thinking around the knowledge dimensions, use this one to organize your thoughts around evidence collection. This organizer is meant to help you understand how you focus your feedback, whether you help create authentic opportunities for collaboration, and understand how you collect evidence in some of our biggest areas of need in schools (e.g., PLCs and faculty meetings).

## Resource 8: Instructional Leadership Graphic Organizer

This is where I would like you to organize your thoughts around the instructional leadership umbrella. In the book you read my definition of instructional leadership. Would you use that definition or create your own? In the top box extend my thinking on instructional leadership or create your own.

In the bottom boxes, write down one way you practice instructional leadership, and one new strategy you learned that you would be willing to try.

# Why This Book?

When I was hired to be a school principal, it was one of the greatest times in my life. I had no leadership experience, had been teaching at a high-poverty city school, and was hired to be the principal of a small rural-suburban school district. We were considered rural because of where we were located in New York State, and we were considered suburban based on the size of our student population.

For the first five years it was the best job of my life, but after 2010–2011 I realized things were changing rapidly. New York State, like many other states and many countries around the world, experienced increased mandates and accountability. Not only were we required to tie a point scale to each of our teacher observations, but high-stakes tests were tied to teacher evaluation as well. Managing these new levels of accountability was a learning experience. I learned about pressure, political agendas, and what happens when the philosophy of the school leader doesn't always mesh with the philosophy of the district, the state, or the nation. It was in this season that I found my true leadership voice.

I was one of eight principals to write a letter to the state education department to argue that high-stakes testing should never be tied to teacher evaluations. I also published many respectful, yet poignant, articles on my *Finding Common Ground* blog for Education Week focusing on why most of the accountability measures were hurting our schools. I also wrote about my understanding that the accountability measures were a consequence of having school leaders who were not necessarily doing what was best for students. However, I found that we leaders simply did not have the time to focus on instruction and meet the demands of this increased accountability. Add on budget cuts and absorbing the whole population of a one-classroom-per-grade-level school that was closed, and we were met with a perfect storm.

Unfortunately, that is when our administrative team began to fracture. Many of us, and many other leaders around the area, talked about how terrible the changes were behind closed doors, but when I went upstate to speak out about them, I felt as though I was standing alone. Fortunately, I had strong support from administrators in western New York and Long Island.

Leadership isn't about standing behind closed doors complaining about accountability and then going to school and making teachers do it. Leadership is about going against the grain and using your voice to speak up about the things that you believe are harmful to learning. If you are against high-stakes testing, say so. If you think high-stakes testing is necessary, then say that. Leadership is about using your voice, even if it means going up against others. It is hard, but it is very, very worth it.

This book is about striking a balance between doing the things you have to do and finding a way to do the things you want to do. Instructional leadership is about focusing a little bit of your time as many days as possible on student learning. Not only is it vitally important for students, but teachers deserve a leader who respects them and wants to stand side-by-side with them. We live in complicated times, and leadership is a challenging but worthwhile calling. I was a better leader because of my teachers and students, even when the going got tough with other leaders around me. As Warren Bennis said many years ago, "Stand up and be a leader." This book will help you do just that.

We often talk about instructional leadership in our educational circles. At universities, in workshops, inspiring keynotes, and through blogs and articles, leaders are told that instructional leadership has an enormous impact on students. In John Hattie's synthesis of meta-analyses, which included more than 400 studies on the topic of leadership, instructional leadership had an effect size of .42. That is higher than the hinge point of .40, which represents a year's worth of growth for a year's input. The problem is that leaders cannot always find the time to focus on instruction and student learning and in some cases were never given practical leadership training. Instructional leadership is one of the most researched forms of leadership in the past 50 years, but it is still as clear as mud because it is difficult to pin down specific, consistent ways of putting it into practice. We are going to work all of that out and clear all of that mud as we make our way through this book together.

In a 10-year study by the National Association of Elementary School Principals (NAESP), Fuller, Young, Richardson, Pendola, and Winn (2018, p. 1) found that the demands of instructional leadership are increasing:

> Over the past few years, the extent to which [the typical principal] uses assessment data for instructional planning has increased, along with her involvement in helping teachers use effective instructional practice and her efforts to develop the school as a professional learning community. She spends much of her time in contact with staff, especially in her supervisory role.

The researchers (2018, p. 2) also cite areas in which leadership is getting more complicated these days when they add that principals' "awareness and involvement have increased dramatically regarding student mental health and student socioemotional awareness."

Instructional leadership is not often broken down into its finest parts, so many leaders may use the term "instructional leadership" but not really know what it is or how to do it. In education, we have a common language and use terms like "growth mindset," "differentiated instruction," and "multiple intelligences," but we often lack a common understanding of those same terms. This book is about defining a common language and a common understanding of instructional leadership.

Instructional leadership is not merely getting out of your office more often and doing walkthroughs or learning walks that provide one-sided feedback. Instructional leadership is when those in a leadership position focus on implementing practices that will increase student learning.

> Instructional leadership is when those in a leadership position focus their efforts on the implementation of practices that will positively impact student learning.

Instructional leadership is about understanding how to implement improvements effectively, build collective efficacy during that implementation process, and work together with teachers and staff to build a focus on learning, so that we can improve our teaching strategies and increase student engagement. Instructional leadership is also about collecting evidence to understand our impact as leaders and practitioners.

This collective work has an enormous impact on student learning. Due to all of these moving parts that include students and teachers working together, we know that instructional leadership is a complicated leadership experience because it is merely one part of what leaders do every day. Yet, many leaders still are eager to learn how to improve their practice.

In that same NAESP study, Fuller et al. (2018, p. 2) found that although the typical principal has increased her capacity and responsibilities significantly, she

> still feels she has much to learn, [and] the areas in which she would most like to receive assistance in improving her abilities are [1] improving student performance, [2] improving staff performance, and [3] school improvement planning. . . . She is most likely to participate in school- and district-provided professional development as opposed to other professional development opportunities.

Here is the issue, though: Many times, that professional development is about mandates and accountability, or it is very teacher-centered.

Unfortunately, a great deal of professional development is not about how to improve as instructional leaders. So, our average school leader expresses a need for support in improving student and staff performance, but she does not engage in professional development opportunities that will give her the tools she needs.

Since the publication of research around instructional leadership, many challenges have surfaced for building- and district-level leaders, as well as for teachers and staff members. Education departments around the world have focused on test scores due to pressure around PISA (Program for International Student Assessment), and schools have had to deal with budget cuts, increased accountability measures, board members who have a singular focus, and a higher number of students who experience trauma and mental health issues. What this means is that the focus of instructional leadership has been blurred by so many pressing issues within the school community, issues trickling down from the district office, and pressures from the state and federal government. Leaders find themselves boxed into a corner of compliance around those accountability measures and mandates and the social-emotional needs of staff members and students. Is there any wonder why instructional leadership is so difficult?

Leaders don't always know how to sort all of these issues out and put their instructional leadership skills into practice. Many leaders feel as though they simply don't have the time, because they are tasked with so many other responsibilities.

Leaders are stressed out, and they are leaving the profession at a breakneck pace. I'd like to try to change that, and I believe that the conversations around instructional leadership need a reboot. That reboot starts with six areas that I have found to be central to instructional leadership: (1) implementation, (2) a focus on learning, (3) student engagement, (4) instructional strategies, (5) collective efficacy and (6) evaluating our impact. Yet, it is rare for any of these six areas to be addressed in publications focusing on instructional leadership.

### Six Areas Instructional Leaders Focus On

1. Implementation
2. Learning
3. Student engagement
4. Instructional strategies
5. Collective efficacy
6. Evaluating our impact

As you make your way through the book, you will notice "Mindful Moment" headings throughout each chapter. I am an avid practitioner of meditation and believe we all need to learn to take moments out of our busy days just to breathe and reflect. The book will provide those moments for you.

*Instructional Leadership: Creating Practice Out of Theory* offers readers the research behind instructional leadership, balanced by practical steps toward becoming instructional leaders. Instructional leadership is one of more than 251 influences John Hattie has researched, and one of the most important, because it provides us with the opportunity to find our voices as leaders and have an impact on student learning.

As a former school principal who now conducts workshops and coaches leaders, I have come to learn that what the research implies that leaders should do and what leaders are *able* to do are sometimes two different things. Let's take the time to change that.

## THIS BOOK'S FEATURES

- **Author Videos**—I have provided an introductory video for each chapter, providing context and highlighting main themes.
- **Program Logic Models**—This feature will help readers define their outcome and the necessary steps to achieve that outcome.
- **Implementation Cycle**—Throughout the book there will be examples of implementation cycles that can be used for instructional leadership practices.
- **Mindful Moments**—School leadership is stressful. Throughout the book, these sections help leaders step back, take a breath, and reflect on their practices.
- **Student Voice Questions**—In each chapter, these questions will help readers reflect on interactions and engagement with students.
- **Study Guide Questions**—At the end of each chapter are questions readers can use as a study guide. I often find that groups read the book together for book clubs, leadership PLCs, and university courses. I will offer questions to help guide those discussions.
- **Instructional Leadership Reflection Framework**—At the end of this book is a reflection framework, which will help guide readers' level of involvement in each of the instructional leadership components.

# Publisher's Acknowledgments

Corwin gratefully acknowledges the contributions of the following individuals:

Anika Blackmore
Principal
Hamersley, Western Australia

Ray Boyd
Principal
Beechboro, Western Australia

Karen Tichy
Assistant Professor of Educational Leadership
St. Louis University

# About the Author

 **Peter M. DeWitt, EdD** is a former K–5 teacher (11 years) and principal (8 years). He runs workshops and provides keynotes nationally and internationally focusing on leadership, coaching, and fostering inclusive school climates. Within North America, his work has been adopted at the university and state levels, and he works with numerous districts, school boards, and regional and state organizations to train leadership teams and coach building leaders.

He is the author of *Collaborative Leadership: Six Influences That Matter Most* (Corwin Press/Learning Forward, 2016), *School Climate: Leading With Collective Efficacy* (Corwin Press/Ontario Principals Council, 2017), *Coach It Further: Using the Art of Coaching to Improve School Leadership* (Corwin Press, 2018), and *Instructional Leadership: Inspiring Practice From Theory* (Corwin Press, 2019).

Along with a team of consultants, school leaders and coaches, he trains educators on collaborative leadership, school coaching and specifically instructional leadership.

His articles have appeared in education journals at the state, national and international level, and he has presented at forums, conferences, and panel discussions at state, national and international conferences, including for the National Association of Elementary School Principals (NAESP), ASCD and NBC's Education Nation.

# Introduction

Have you ever tried to go on one of the popular diets out there? Whether we are on social media or sitting back watching television at night, we are exposed to what seems like countless diets. Some ask us to cut out carbs, some tell us to cut out sugar and some prohibit foods containing flour. Some of them ask us to fast for 16 hours a day. What I have often found is that these diets give quick results, but we cannot maintain such eating habits for a long time. We cannot sustain diets that ask us to cut out so much of what we eat, because at the first feeling of frustration we will go back to old habits. Even when we are excited about the prospect of losing weight, we have those moments that take us two steps forward and one step back, and that's when we are on the verge of collapse.

Over the last couple of years, I have turned to a healthier way to live. It began when I started looking at photos of myself that people shared on social media, and I thought the photos made me look heavy. So many times I chalked it up to a bad photo or a bad angle. I soon realized it was not the photo and that I was no longer looking like the long-distance runner I used to be so many years ago. So, I talked with a few friends who lived healthy lives and began to change small areas that had led to my weight gain. I cut down on snacks. Instead of doing the elliptical machine for 30 minutes five times a week, I bumped it up to 60 minutes five or six times a week. I began practicing meditation every morning and every night, because I found that some of my unhealthy habits, like drinking too much red wine, were triggered by the anxiety and stress I was feeling. After a few months of meditation, I cut out red wine and cut down on drinking overall. Over the last year and a half, I changed my habits one small step at a time and ultimately lost 35 pounds. I hadn't signed on to a miracle diet; instead, I had taken a much more holistic approach to changing my lifestyle. Now I am much healthier, I don't need as much prescription medication for my aging body, and my mind is much more clear. I have been able to keep going on this much healthier path for two years.

The research around instructional leadership is much like the information we see online around diets. Fads, shiny new toys found on social media, and prescriptive guidelines of "don't do this—do that" abound, but many times such approaches lead to change that doesn't last, and then we find ourselves going back to old habits. The heavy weight of our jobs returns like the pounds we once thought we had shed forever.

That doesn't seem healthy. I prefer a much more holistic approach to instructional leadership, where we can make small changes that will persist for a long time. The teachers and students around us are tired of quick fixes that never last. They deserve more from us. That means we must invest in collaborating with our staff and work on improvements that may take a year or two to achieve. Yes, instructional leadership and improvement can have short-term benefits, but we need to make sure we focus on long-term commitments as well.

Instructional leadership is a topic that I have long been interested in. We have all had great times in our lives that we remember fondly. One of those times for me was when I was teaching at a high-poverty elementary school in the city while also completing my degree in school administration, doing a 600-hour internship as part of that degree, and teaching as an adjunct professor at the same university I was attending. Yes, my life was busy, but I had a supportive partner, and it was one of the most influential learning experiences in my life. During that crazy period, I was taking a Critical Issues course from 4:00 p.m. to 7:15 and then teaching a course from 7:30 to 10:00, and that was after a full day of teaching and putting in internship hours.

It may sound overwhelming, and perhaps it was (a little), but I was living through a time when I was completely enveloped by leadership and watching how it transferred to the students in my elementary classroom, the graduate course I was teaching, and my administrative internship. That desire to learn more about leadership continued to drive me over the eight years of my role as a building leader and the last five years of my consultancy and independent research.

## Mindful Moment

Take a moment to reflect on how you entered into school leadership. Who inspired you? Why did you want to become a leader?

Keep that inspiration close to you as you negotiate your way through this book.

I believe it is that passion for leadership, and my need to try to figure it all out as I work with leaders who come from very diverse backgrounds and are working through a wide variety of issues, that has led me to enter into my own phase of educational research. But here's the thing: The research alone will not make instructional leadership happen. Understanding practices is not enough; we need knowledge around implementation and a commitment to our practices, which is where I see a continuing issue with instructional leadership.

Sometimes a lack of strong instructional leadership practices is due to leaders' need to stay in the role of manager, and other times it is because they don't know where to start as an instructional leader, even after all the theory they learned in their leadership training. After all, some of the research on instructional leadership was published before leaders began to face so many pieces of accountability and mandates, and a lot of it was certainly published before leaders had to work with teachers to find a balance between students' academic and their social-emotional learning.

For one reason or another, many leaders seem to operate in perpetual crisis mode, which prevents them from entering into classrooms as often as they would like to. Their district leaders pull them out of the school several times a week for meetings, professional development that is often geared toward sit-and-get compliance issues, or, ironically, to cover other buildings because that leader is out. Yes, leaders are called out of their buildings to deal with discipline issues in other buildings because that principal is out of district. And we wonder why instructional leadership seems so elusive.

As a leadership coach, I have worked with principals who have to deal with gang activity, students who are being trafficked for sex, homeless students, drug abuse, and many other extreme issues. If we want to talk about instructional leadership, then we also have to have an open discussion about such issues, yet very few leadership researchers bring those topics up at all.

In preparation for this book, I have been doing research around instructional leadership. I sent out surveys that were completed by close to one thousand general and special education teachers, instructional coaches, and school principals. Additionally, I completed one-on-one interviews with teachers and principals. What I have found is that leaders are so busy putting out fires, so to speak, that they don't often enough get the opportunity to be proactive. They rarely have a chance to deepen their understanding of instruction and student learning.

My research shows that many principals believe they are instructional leaders, but many teachers don't share that view. Some of that discrepancy around instructional leadership has to do with proximity. Teachers only believe what they can see. If a principal practices instructional leadership and teachers don't see it, did it really happen?

I have the good fortune to meet and work with many researchers in the field of education, and I have taken the opportunity to do my own research as well. Many of the people I work with have done outstanding research on educational leadership or instructional leadership. In fact, while writing this book I was in Edinburgh, Scotland, and spent time with Michael Fullan, Viviane Robinson, John Hattie, Shirley Clarke, and Jenni Donohoo. Through their words, feedback, and insight, all of these individuals helped me shape what you are about to read.

Sometimes, though, the actions that researchers recommend don't fit with what leaders can actually do. Is that because many of the researchers were never in a leadership position themselves? Maybe. Is it because the research is great but leaders never have the time to read it in depth? That is definitely part of the issue. It's also because researchers may focus on best practices at a time when leaders do not always have the opportunity to focus on those best practices.

## TAP INTO YOUR TRUE INNER INSTRUCTIONAL LEADER

We need a starting point, and that starting point may look very different for each and every leader reading this book. It is not enough to just call ourselves "instructional leaders" or "lead learners." In fact, it's important that we stop using the term "instructional leader" if, in fact, we aren't practicing instructional leadership, because misusing the phrase chips away at our school climates and our own credibility. Teachers and students certainly get tired of our actions not matching up with our words. This discrepancy between claims and actions is a topic that I have focused on many times before, including in the following blog post (DeWitt, 2014a), which I think best illustrates my point.

---

### Help! My Principal Says He's an Instructional Leader!

*To me, instructional leadership is not about the leader at all but about how the leader works as a team with their students, staff and parents to put the focus on learning.*

What works? What doesn't? What is the new fad? What are the tried and true methods that have always worked?

In these days of quick fixes and fast moving initiatives, we spend most of our time at the surface level. We look at numbers and sometimes make rash decisions.

We read a blog, article or book and quickly believe what we read will solve our problems, only to find we had surface level knowledge and the fix was more of a distraction.

Although we know reflection is important in what we do, we often don't do it until something goes wrong. Even with our best intentions, our haste makes waste when we try to solve our issues without having a true understanding of what they are and how to use the "fix" properly. This happens in leadership all the time.

One of the focal points of educational leadership is that of the difference between transformational leadership and instructional leadership. Long ago when I was knee-deep in a leadership program, transformational leadership was all the rage. Over the past few years though, some researchers have pointed out that transformational leadership has a smaller effect size than instructional leadership (see Petty, n.d.).

According to leadership expert Viviane Robinson, the effect size of transformational leadership is .11 while the effect size of instructional leadership is .42. In his several decades of research John Hattie has found that anything over a .40 (Hinge Point) can provide at least a year's growth in a year's time.

And this is where weak leadership can ruin the effects of instructional leadership. . . .

It's easy to get caught up in the numbers. Principals, new or old, read the effect size literature and note that instructional leadership can have an impact on student growth, so they begin walking into classrooms all the time. Without the proper mindset, knowledge of instruction, and prep work done with staff, leaders are in jeopardy of using the right term (instructional leadership) while doing it the wrong way.

And teachers and students are the ones on the receiving end of the out-of-control swinging pendulum.

**Going Deeper . . .**

I once read a tweet by a teacher who said, "It irritates me every time I see my administrator walk in with his iPad." As much as that may be an arrogant statement on the part of the teacher, they may have had many reasons for feeling irritated. What if their administrator liked to document everything and tell the teacher what they were doing wrong but lacked the instructional knowledge to really offer effective feedback?

If school leaders do not involve teachers in the process of being an instructional leader, they're really not leading at all. Leaders need to offer clarity of what instructional leadership looks like, and to do this correctly they need to make sure they are

*(Continued)*

(Continued)

asking teachers for their input. What do teachers want out of instructional leadership? To be left alone is not acceptable. Teachers can really offer guidance of what good instruction looks like, and instructional leaders know that and have a lot of dialogue around it.

Leaders need to not only read the latest research but become familiar with practical examples of how to be an effective instructional leader. In doing their research of the philosophical and the practical, they need to also make sure that they are using building structures like faculty meetings, Principal Advisory Council and student focus groups to make sure they are sharing (and hearing!) best practices and keeping the focus on learning.

Being an instructional leader is more than just saying they are the lead learner, but it's about acting accordingly. It's not just the words that leaders use but how they act and what they model. It's about using the expert teachers around them to model great instruction.

To me, instructional leadership is not about the leader at all but about how the leader works as a team with their students, staff and parents to put the focus on learning.

### Characteristics of an Instructional Leader

Viviane Robinson says, "While there is considerable evidence about the impact of instructional leadership on student outcomes, there is far less known about the leadership capabilities that are required to confidently engage in the practices involved (2010, p. 1)."

Robinson outlines the characteristics needed for leaders to be instructional leaders. They are:

- **Leadership Content Knowledge**—Robinson says, "Their (Nelson & Sassi) research showed that as leaders gained a deeper understanding of what is involved in effective teaching of particular curriculum areas, they were able to detect and correct mismatches between those understandings and the administrative routines that were intended to support them."

- **Solving Complex Problems**—Robinson says, "Experts in their field use problem-solving processes that are distinguishable from those of less expert performers and that expertise is inextricably linked with that discussed in the first capability—leadership content knowledge."

- **Building Relational Trust**—Robinson says, "The importance of relationships is evident from the fact that leadership is, by definition, a social process. Leadership is attributed to those members of a group or organization who are seen to influence others in ways that advance the group or organization's progress toward its goals (Katz & Kahn, 1966; Robinson, 2010)."

## In the End

Sometimes leaders work in the very silos that they accuse teachers of living in. Being an instructional leader is vitally important, but making sure that it is being done correctly is even more important. Saying and doing are two different things. Teachers are the ones who never left the classroom, and instructional leaders are the ones who make it a point to go into those classrooms as often as possible (every day!), but going into the classroom isn't enough. We need to go deeper, and it takes the conversations before, during and after those classroom visits to bring us there.

## References

Katz, D., & Kahn, R. L. (1978). *The social psychology of organizations* (2nd ed.). New York, NY: Wiley.

Nelson, B. S., & Sassi, A. (2005). *The effective principal: Instructional leadership for high-quality learning* (Critical Issues in Educational Leadership series). New York, NY: Teachers College Press.

Petty, G. (n.d.). Research and links. http://geoffpetty.com/for-team-leaders/research-and-links/

Robinson, V. M. J. (2010). Instructional leadership to leadership capabilities: Empirical findings and methodological challenges. *Leadership and Policy in Schools, 9*(1), 1–26.

Day, Gu, and Sammons (2016, p. 222) found that a "school's abilities to improve and sustain effectiveness over the long term are not primarily the result of the principal's leadership style but of their understanding and diagnosis of the school's needs." Throughout this book, I will take the research around instructional leadership and make it practical for you to go deeper with instructional leadership practices that will help you understand the needs of your school.

Day et al. (2016, p. 222) go on to say that to sustain effectiveness over the long term, which should be the goal of all leaders, leaders must spend time creating an "application of clearly articulated, organizationally shared educational values through multiple combinations and accumulations of time and context-sensitive strategies that are 'layered' and progressively embedded in the school's work, culture, and achievements." No more fad diets, just slow and long-lasting improvement.

This book is about addressing the research and understanding where to start, because we need leaders like you. I don't want that passion you entered into your leadership degree with to fizzle out during your first years in the role. However, I also want to make sure that if you refer to yourself as an "instructional leader," you are actually doing the work to back it up.

# INSTRUCTIONAL LEADERSHIP

## A Holistic Approach

Collective Efficacy

Evidence

Instructional Strategies

Implementation

Student Engagement

A Focus on Learning

Scan this QR code for a video introduction to the chapter.

Over the last six years, I have conducted workshops; delivered keynote speeches; created a multi-day competency-based course around collaborative leadership that has been adopted at the state and university levels; and been coaching the same elementary, middle-, and high-school principals for over two years. The first influence out of the six that I explored in my book *Collaborative Leadership: Six Influences That Matter Most* was that of instructional leadership, which is a direct focus on teaching and learning. After teaching the six influences and all the research and nuances that come with implementing each one, I found that I was often asked back to work with leaders on instructional leadership. It happened once, and I enjoyed going deeper into that form of leadership. However, it began to happen again and again, and that's when I realized that there must be some unanswered questions around the research. Why else would there be so much interest?

As I have met and presented for so many school leaders (i.e., instructional coaches, teacher leaders, building and district leaders), I have had the opportunity to survey several hundred leaders, teachers, and instructional coaches, as well as interview dozens of leaders. All of this work originated in North America but has branched out to Europe, the United Kingdom, and Australia.

What I have found is that many leaders both nationally and internationally want to be instructional leaders, and so many of them do an outstanding job in the role, but others are desperately looking for a place to start. Instructional leadership is when those in a leadership position focus on implementing practices that will increase student learning. I believe strongly that through research and experience, I have found the necessary components of instructional leadership that will help guide leaders through that role.

When we understand effective implementation processes, we build collective efficacy and work together to develop common understandings of learning concepts. That collective efficacy and those common understandings will improve our teaching strategies and have a positive impact on student learning, and we can collect evidence to understand that impact. I believe this can be a powerful way for those in leadership positions to practice instructional leadership.

---

### Instructional leaders focus on:

- Implementation
- Learning
- Student engagement

- Instructional strategies
- Efficacy
- Evaluation of impact

Focusing on the six areas I have identified will help leaders work alongside teachers to set a clear, practical, and impactful vision for quality instruction, which will help them continually place a focus on learning.

The idea of putting a focus on learning in school may sound like common sense, but too often the focus in our schools centers around the adults more than the students (Hattie, 2015). This focus on adult issues can take so much time that leaders don't even clearly understand how much time they are taking to talk about union issues, prep time, student discipline that may have resulted from an uninspiring lesson, or conversations with parents around a lack of communication from their child's teacher. All of those real-world problems (a) prevent leaders from getting into classrooms to focus on instructional practices and (b) force them to rush through formal observations and conversations with teachers, which does not build their credibility as an instructional leader. In fact, many leaders surveyed believe they are instructional leaders, but many teachers who answered the same survey do not feel the same way about their leaders (DeWitt, 2019).

////////////////////////////////////////////////////////////////////////

## Student Voice Questions

How do you encourage student voice in the learning that takes place in your school?

Are students represented in stakeholder groups? Not as tokens so that the adults can *say* students have a voice, but real, authentic opportunities for students to share their voices?

////////////////////////////////////////////////////////////////////////

Figure 1.1 shows the results of a survey that I did in 2019. In the small-scale survey involving more than 300 building leaders and 300 teachers, 67% of leaders (principals) said they were either confident (43%) or very confident (24%) that they were instructional leaders; 25% said they were somewhat confident; and only 8% said they were not confident in this regard.

However, teachers did not reflect the same levels of confidence about their principals being instructional leaders. While 67% of leaders reported feeling confident or very confident, only 38% of teachers said they were confident or very confident that their principal was an instructional leader. Another 32% were somewhat confident in their principal's ability to be an instructional leader. Nearly one third (30%) of teachers confessed to a lack of confidence in their principal's ability to be an instructional leader (DeWitt, 2019).

**Figure 1.1**   Leaders' Perspective vs. Teachers' Perspective

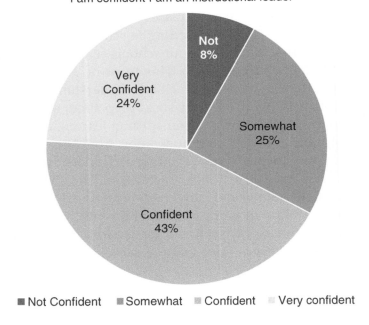

I am confident I am an instructional leader

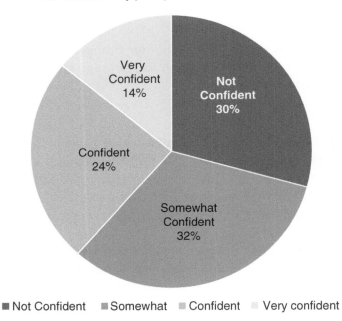

I am confident my principal is an instructional leader

**Mindful Moment**

Reflect on the discrepancy between leaders' and teachers' responses to the instructional leadership survey. How would the teachers you work with answer the survey question? Sometimes leaders have an inflated view of their instructional leadership practices, while teachers do not see their leaders often enough in classrooms, so they have a less generous view.

Complete the following sentence.

As a leader, I:

A. know what I'm talking about and can follow through.
B. know what I'm talking about, but I don't communicate that fact effectively.
C. think I know what I'm talking about, but teachers don't believe it.
D. know what I should be focusing on but can't do it as much as I would like to.
E. don't know where to begin.

Take a step back and think about whether you should explore this issue. One way is to administer a building-specific survey in which teachers can anonymously provide their thoughts to you, their leader. Additionally, you can share the pie charts in Figure 1.1 at a faculty meeting. Please just keep in mind that teachers will not speak truthfully if they do not trust their leader.

Believe it or not, a leader may be seen as an instructional leader by some teachers but not others in the same building. The leader in question may spend more time in certain classrooms because of his or her good relationship with those teachers and have conversations around student engagement or instructional strategies. However, that same leader may spend less time in other classrooms because of a lack of confidence in his or her relationship with those teachers. Those teachers who see their leader most often may believe that he or she is an instructional leader, while those who see the leader least often will not consider that person an instructional leader. What this means is proximity matters. All leaders need to maximize the time they have with all staff members, and that time is best used when it is focused on learning.

**Mindful Moment**

Consider the times that you have proximity to all staff in your building. Whether you are a building leader, a teacher leader or an instructional coach, do you have access to all staff members for equal amounts of time? How do you spend that time? Is there a focus on learning? Answering this question is not a time for confirmation bias. Please don't quickly answer, "Of course I focus on learning!" Seek out the opinion of a few of your staff members.

An interesting issue with instructional leadership is that many new leaders come to the position with teaching experience, but they leave that experience at the door because they believe they have somehow gone to the "dark side." They abandon their former lives as teachers in an effort to dive into their new life as a principal or other leader. Other times, leaders are not as keen on teaching as they are on management, so they spend their time focusing on their management responsibilities. This begins to spiral into spending more time in their office checking e-mails; attending administrator meetings scheduled by their district or their regional or state education department; meeting with students to wade through discipline issues; and meeting with families to work out communication issues with teachers. All of this makes it difficult for them to focus on large-scale consistent improvement in the buildings they lead.

/////////////////////////////////////////////////////////////////////

## Student Voice Questions

If your students were asked to answer a similar survey regarding instructional leadership, what would their answers look like? Let's make an assumption that students understand that an instructional leader is someone who enters classrooms and talks with students about learning. Would your students see you as an instructional leader?

/////////////////////////////////////////////////////////////////////

Elmore (2000, p. 20) provides five principles to help leaders focus on the large-scale improvements they desire:

- The purpose of leadership is the improvement of instructional practice and performance, regardless of role.
- Instructional improvement requires continuous learning: Learning is both an individual and a social activity.
- Learning requires modeling: Leaders must lead by modeling the values and behavior that represent collective goods.
- The roles and activities of leadership flow from the expertise required for learning and improvement, not from the formal dictates of the institution.
- The exercise of authority requires reciprocity of accountability and capacity.

These five principles are not easily made evident, especially by leaders who have not built credibility in their role. Leaders who try to dive into the five principles without first building credibility can create major misunderstandings within their school community.

**Mindful Moment**

Think of an instance when you tried to improve your instructional practice at school or made an improvement in your personal life.

What did that feel like to accomplish?

Too often we forget those moments. Think of how they helped make you the person you are today.

These misunderstandings are not just an issue in the United States; they happen in countries around the world, including those that are often seen as providing a more robust educational experience to students. Too many leaders are so busy in their management role that they cannot find time to focus on their role as instructional leader. This constant cycle of moving forward without deep thinking can create stress, especially when it's happening in a district where principals feel like their schools are in competition with each other. Salo, Nylund, and Stjernstrøm found that "school leadership practices, even though they are played out quite differently in relation to the various national contexts and local traditions, have been affected by the global discourses of competition and accountability" (2015, p. 494).

For many principals, in the blink of an eye, the life they once had as teachers in the classroom seems so very long ago. Instructional leadership is about finding a balance and weaving that teaching experience into your practices as a principal. I know what you are wondering: What if I didn't start out as a classroom teacher? Can I be an instructional leader if I wasn't a teacher first? What does that mean for me? It means that you will have to work equally as hard with your staff to prove your credibility as an instructional leader, because you may not have teaching experience to draw on.

Principals who did not begin as a classroom teacher—who instead had experience as a school psychologist, as a counselor, or in some other role—can use that unique experience to provide a different perspective on students and mix it in with the best practices of an instructional leader. Instructional leadership isn't about always having the right answers; it's about asking the right questions, and it often begins with how you implement improvements in your school.

## What the Research Says About Instructional Leadership

Edmonds (1979) began researching instructional leadership in the late 1970s in mostly high-poverty urban settings. The research suggests that instructional leadership includes practices aimed at fostering teachers' professional learning and growth, as well as facilitating work around teacher and building goals, school climate, and implementing curriculum in classrooms and grade levels that will ultimately have an impact on student engagement (Robinson, Lloyd, & Rowe, 2008, pp. 638–639; Southworth, 2002, pp. 76–86; Salo et al., 2015, p. 491). Additionally, research shows that leadership practices have a strong impact on student learning both directly and indirectly (Kruger, Witziers, & Sleegers, 2007).

Unfortunately, there is not much research focusing on specific ways to put instructional leadership into practice. Salo et al. (2015) highlighted this deficiency, saying, "Despite the emphasis on the effects of school leadership regarding teaching practices and learning outcomes, research on direct instructional leadership is scarce." The researchers have referred to instructional leadership as a sort of black box: "Not much is known about why, when and how principals guide teachers' work in the classroom" (Salo et al., 2015, p. 490).

Rigby (2014, p. 611) described the lack of data as a problem of details: "Currently, there is no characterization in either the practice or research leadership literature that outlines the various ways in which instructional leadership is presented in the institutional environment." To Elmore (2000), a good definition of "instructional leadership" seemed so hard to find that he called it "the holy grail in educational administration" (p. 7).

Leithwood, Louis, Anderson, and Wahlstrom (2004, p. 3) stated: "While evidence about leadership effects on student learning can be confusing to interpret, much of the existing research actually underestimates its effects. The total (direct and indirect) effects of leadership on student learning account for about a quarter of total school effects." However, the researchers warned: "The term 'instructional leader' has been in vogue for decades as the desired model for education leaders—principals especially. Yet the term is often more a slogan than a well-defined set of leadership practices." Leithwood et al. (2004) went on to say, "It is no more meaningful, in and of itself, than admonishing the leader of any organization to keep his or her eye on the organizational 'ball.'" This is one of the reasons that I wanted to introduce you to the implementation model before we move on to any real discussion focusing on instructional leadership.

During their research, Hallinger and Heck (1996) found that instructional leadership was the most commonly researched form of school leadership, which illustrates the high level of interest in the topic. Hallinger has long been one of the most notable researchers when it comes to instructional leadership. He has broken the practice of instructional leadership down into three categories, each with many components (2005, p. 5).

## Hallinger's Three Categories of Instructional Leadership

1. Defining the school mission
2. Managing the instructional program
3. Creating a positive school climate

### Mindful Moment

Does your school mission focus on learning? Is the word "learning" in your mission statement? If so, it makes it easier to focus on the instructional program and creating a positive school climate.

## Rigby's Three Forms of Logic Behind Instructional Leadership

**Prevailing logic:** The role of the principal is to be both an instructional leader and manager of the school site.

**Entrepreneurial logic:** The focus of instructional leadership is to alter inequitable outcomes through innovation and mechanisms from the private sector. It rejects the traditional training of education schools and a model that includes multiple and flexible approaches.

**Social justice logic:** Focused on the experiences and inequitable outcomes of marginalized groups (Rigby, 2014)

## Moving From Theory to Practice

It is easy to research and talk about instructional leadership, and even easier to debate its nuances, but much harder to put it into practice. Implementing improvements takes a great deal of time and research if you want to do it right, and principals do not always feel like they have the time—or they simply don't care to take the time—to do that.

What makes leadership so difficult is that we do not always approach it with the right mindset. We dive into our perceived improvement before we even know why we are diving in. At the Visible Learning World Conference in Edinburgh, Scotland, in March 2019, renowned leadership researcher and professor Viviane Robinson said it best when she stated, "Don't design the future until you deeply understand the present." Some of that understanding means diving into the research about the improvement you want to implement. Sadly, I have found that most leaders and teachers do not take the time to study the improvement enough before they dive into the implementation.

We know that all the managerial aspects to the job mentioned above make practicing instructional leadership difficult for school principals, but all schools need their principals to spend some of their time, even if it's one quarter of their time at first, in the role of instructional leader.

## Mindful Moment

Reflect on your day. Do you have 30 minutes in your day to spend in classrooms? Many times leaders spend time in classrooms but bring their laptop or phone with them, even though the time spent in the classroom is not for an observation. This means they're distracted from what's going on in front of them. Start by disconnecting, and spend 30 minutes in several of your most inspiring classrooms. It will help you remember why you love education.

Fullan and Quinn (2016) correctly stated that leaders at "system, district, and school levels need to influence the culture and processes that support learning and working together in purposeful ways" (p. 53). The authors went on to write that policymakers at the state and district levels made a mistake in positioning principals in the role of instructional leader. Fullan and Quinn write that those policymakers "overinterpreted the research that the principal was the second (to the teacher) most important source of learning for students and proceeded to position the principal as conducting classroom visits, performing teacher appraisals, and taking corresponding action to develop or get rid of teachers" (p. 53). They pointed out that there is not enough time in the day for leaders to move forward this way given their other responsibilities, and those leaders need, instead, to focus on being a "lead learner," which would indirectly influence each teacher, and to focus on human capital.

I believe we need to take that important work of Fullan and Quinn and find a balance between a focus on human capital and a focus on being an instructional leader. After all, whether we refer to a principal as a "lead learner" or the "instructional leader," the word "lead" is always involved. Taking a leadership position means taking the responsibility to move a building forward. We just need to make sure we are working collaboratively in order to do it, because the teachers we work with may have a higher level of expertise than we do. We should learn from them in the same way we want them to learn from us.

## In the End

Research on instructional leadership has been around for decades, but it is often so diverse in its findings that it doesn't always help building principals become instructional leaders. Over the last five years, I have worked closely with researchers, some of whom will be cited in this book, and have taken the opportunity to do my own research around instructional leadership because I coach leaders, conduct workshops for them, and have a deep desire to make sure that I blend research with practical strategies that will help them grow.

As I mentioned before, instructional leadership really comes down to six driving forces. Those six areas are implementation, a focus on learning, student engagement, instructional strategies, efficacy, and collecting evidence to understand our impact (DeWitt, 2019). If you are truly going to begin on the path of instructional leadership, you must start by focusing on these six areas.

What I would like to do in the following chapters is take the research—both others' and my own—and define "instructional leadership" in a way that building principals, instructional coaches, and teacher leaders can use. My goal is to bring research and practice together, despite the many challenges to doing that. I will provide practical suggestions on how to move forward, and I hope that I will also challenge some of your beliefs and get you to reflect on your own practices as a leader.

## STUDY GUIDE QUESTIONS

- How do you build credibility as an instructional leader?
- What is the relationship between your level of instructional leadership and the ways students learn in your school?
- How do you incorporate research into your leadership practices?
- Where is there a gap in what the research suggests you do and what you are allowed to do?
- How has social media impacted your leadership practices?
- How do you go about implementing new strategies?
- What evidence does your leadership team collect to understand whether those leadership practices are working?
- Out of the six areas of instructional leadership that were highlighted, and which we will explore deeply in this book, which one will be the starting point for each person on your team?

# 2

# THE LOGIC BEHIND IMPLEMENTATION

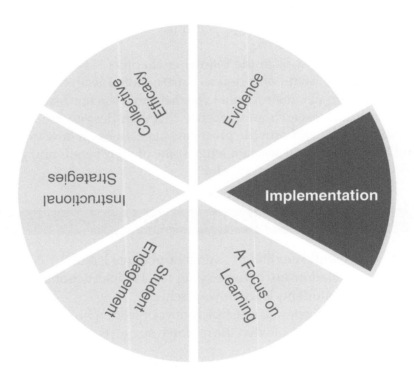

Efficacy

Collective

Instructional

Strategies

Evidence

Implementation

A Focus on

Learning

Student

Engagement

Scan this QR code for a video introduction to the chapter.

Recently, I was working with a group of district leaders in California who were experiencing initiative fatigue. Does that sound familiar? There were too many initiatives being pushed at the same time, and, to make matters worse, most of the leaders were quite new, although a few had leadership experience in other districts. Some had been principals in other districts, but most had very little experience in their current roles.

During a district workshop, we listed the number of initiatives their school district was exploring. We discussed how the numerous initiatives were having a negative impact on the district's functioning. The leaders reported that they had to attend compliance trainings so often that a few of them calculated they spent only about 60% of their time in their school building. The biggest issue besides trust among the group was that they picked initiatives but never stuck to any of them unless they were forced to by the state. And even those initiatives were not necessarily implemented well. The assistant superintendent, who was highly engaged in the workshop discussion, agreed that there were too many initiatives at once. When leaders are under the weight of too many initiatives, it breeds reactive leadership as opposed to proactive leadership.

The story of the leaders in this district is not very different from that of many others I have worked with over the years. Too many initiatives, too little time. And the initiatives they chase don't seem to be worth the time they spend trying to implement them.

### Mindful Moment

Reflect on the number of initiatives that you are responsible for carrying out. I know it's easy to jump to the negative, but let's focus on the positive for just this moment. Which ones are the initiatives that you really like? Which ones do you wish you could dedicate more quality time to?

When it comes to the six components of instructional leadership, let's begin with implementation, because not only is it highly important; if not practiced effectively, it can be detrimental to the progress you would hope to see in your school. For the purpose of the information that follows in the next few paragraphs, I would like you to begin thinking about one initiative that you could devote a little more time to, because I'd really like what you read here to connect to your leadership practices and help you go a bit deeper.

Truth be told, while doing the research for this book, I underestimated how important implementation was until I had an online conversation with Stephen Cox, the CEO of Osiris Educational. Stephen is someone I have partnered with in the past and has become a friend. I was exploring the areas of instructional leadership in my *Finding Common Ground* blog (for *Education Week*) but did not list implementation as one of the main focal points. I was planning on writing about it within each chapter, but I never considered dedicating a full chapter to it. Stephen commented: "Can I add one other area of focus to leaders which has implications for all the others . . . implementation. This is a relatively dormant area both in terms of research and science in the messy context of education. However, it is the gateway to scalability." When I raised the possibility of incorporating implementation into each chapter, he replied: "Implementation is such a complicated theme and is difficult to roll up with the other areas. It requires understanding of linearity at the same time as integration back into the whole. By tackling one implementation at a time, the whole can easily be lost" (personal communication, March 28, 2019).

The conversation was not easily left behind, and as I moved on to run workshops or work with leaders, I could see that most of the issues they were trying to solve came back to poor implementation. Writing, like leadership, is about learning from others, and Stephen definitely helped me realize that implementation is more important than adding on to each chapter.

> ### Mindful Moment
>
> I am sure that, like me, you have had someone lay a few words down in front of you that have changed the course of your career or the way you operate. Who was it? What were the words this person said, and how did they help you improve your practice?

Before we work through program logic, implementation science and other areas, I want to explain why all of this is so vitally important for instructional leaders. There will be many areas of improvement that you want to implement, but poor implementation can kill even the best initiatives. If you do not have a clearly defined reason for doing what you are doing, all will be lost. The other thing to keep in mind is that even the best initiatives have an implementation dip, so let's begin there. After all, the old saying is "you only get one chance to make a first impression," and the same goes for implementation.

At times when implementation doesn't go well, it's often blamed on a resistant teacher, a lack of time, or a bad policy—and there may be a sliver of truth to any of these allegations. If we are to ever move forward, leaders and teachers need to discuss the obstacles that may arise, as well as the reason for the improvement being implemented. Groups also have to discuss that, no matter how important the initiative is, there will always be an *implementation dip.* In *Leading in a Culture of Change* (2007, p. 49), Fullan said:

> [S]uccessful organizations experience implementation dips as they move forward. . . . The implementation dip is a dip in performance and confidence as one engages in an innovation that requires new skills and new understandings.

It's important that all leaders and teachers be familiar with the implementation dip. Fullan goes on to say:

> Leaders who understand the implementation dip know that people are experiencing two kinds of problems when they are in the dip—the social-psychological fear of change and the lack of technical know-how to make the change work (p. 51).

All leaders, but especially those who are focusing on instructional improvements to have a positive impact on student learning, need to understand implementation and the implementation dip. The implementation dip is that moment of cognitive conflict during the improvement process when people question the need for the improvement or aren't sure whether they are putting it into practice correctly. They have to work through their insecurities over abandoning an old practice they felt comfortable with and take time to clearly articulate for themselves the need for the improvement. Additionally, those implementing the improvement have to reflect on and evaluate the implementation at multiple steps, which allows for much-needed dialogue among team members about how the improvement is going.

> Implementation begins with more than just one good idea. It begins with program logic.

We often think of the implementation of initiatives as a school district, macro-level issue, but the reality is that implementation has everything to do with how leaders foster an environment of learning in their schools and how teachers carry out instructional strategies in their classrooms. To be clear, this is not a quick process, which is part of the reason why leaders do not always follow through. In order to implement an initiative well, you need time and plenty of dialogue. Implementation begins with more than just one good idea. It begins with program logic.

////////////////////////////////////////////////////////////////////////

## Student Voice Questions

When you think about the implementation of instructional strategies, or even things as profound as one-to-one initiatives, how are the strategies communicated to students? We know that initiatives can have a big impact on teachers and leaders because of the sheer amount of time they take to implement. Do students feel that impact too?

////////////////////////////////////////////////////////////////////////

## What Is Program Logic?

When we think of initiatives, we do not always view them as logical. In fact, many times we feel as if initiatives keep us from accomplishing other things or that they're just something our central office wants us to get done. Not all initiatives are frivolous, and we need to step back, breathe, and think about the best way to approach them. What is involved in the implementation? Why do we need the initiative? What are the steps we must take to put it in place? This is where program logic comes in.

*Program logic* is a visual representation for leaders and teachers to use when designing and implementing an improvement within their school. Think of it as a concept map for leaders, teachers and staff members to use as a means of working through the issues they seem to be facing. Those issues can, of course, be related to a crisis such as major budget cuts, school consolidations or an achievement gap among students. They can also be about something more learning-focused, such as new grading philosophies, clarity in our common language or levels of learning (e.g., surface, deep and transfer learning). Program logic can be used for initiatives big and small.

> Program logic is a visual representation for leaders and teachers to use when designing and implementing an improvement within their school.

When initiating a program logic model, it's important to meet with the improvement team and discuss the five components of the program logic model. As shown in Figure 2.1, a program logic model involves thinking through our needs, inputs, activities, outputs, and impact.

Keep in mind, though, that program logic models can be mapped out in different ways. They can be as simple as the one in Figure 2.1, or, for those who are much more creative, they can be done in a sketchnoting method, as in Figure 2.2.

### What Is Sketchnoting?

*Sketchnoting* is a way of visually representing ideas by combining notes and sketches. It can help people connect important ideas and concepts or even capture the brainstorming thoughts of a group. The process of sketchnoting certainly fits into the program logic model way of thinking.

As you can see, program logic models include five distinct areas that help us connect to a larger, more impactful idea. The list on page 26 highlights the basic definitions of each component.

**Figure 2.1**    Program Logic Model

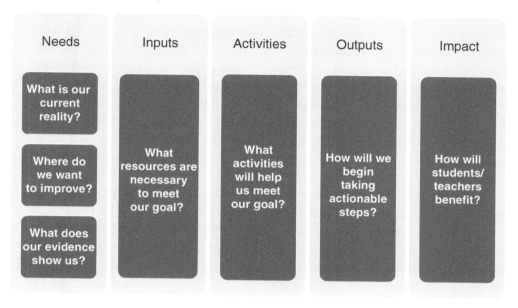

**Figure 2.2**    Example of Sketchnoting

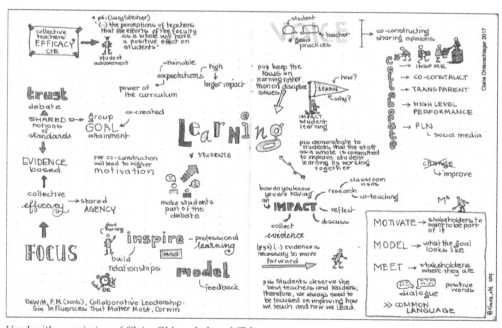

Used with permission of Claire Ohlenschalger, MEd.

**Needs.** What is the area we believe we need to improve upon? This need should not be based on desire to have the latest technology or on a fear of missing out (FOMO)—for example, on the strategies or innovations we see other leaders using on social media. The need addressed here should be decided upon by looking at evidence, having authentic discussions with staff members, and determining where there is a gap in the school's improvement.

**Inputs.** These are resources that we deem necessary to helping us achieve our impact. Resources could be articles, time or whatever we decide we need to achieve our goal. Inputs are definitely important, but we also want to make sure that we do not put so many on the list that it becomes cumbersome.

**Activities.** What activities will help get us there? Walkthroughs, modeling of lessons, co-teaching and flipped faculty meetings can be the activities we use to get us to our impact goal. Unfortunately, some leaders do not truly understand why they are doing walkthroughs or flipped faculty meetings, so they view them as outcomes or impact. Nothing could be further from the truth. Impact is about the improvement we want to see as a school community, and the activity helps get us there. Just as with inputs, it's important not to create too many activities, because then the process becomes overwhelming.

**Outputs.** What steps will we take first? Often in their lives, people remain in the pre-contemplative stage of change. They think about making improvements, but they do not realize the ways in which they can begin right now. Going back to the diet analogy from the introduction, it's like thinking about getting healthy as you take another bite of a double cheeseburger. Outputs are about putting down the cheeseburger and putting one foot in front of the other. Outputs are about actually taking the steps (double meaning intended) needed to get us to improvement. An example would be, "I will flip the October faculty meeting," and not just, "One of these days I will flip a faculty meeting."

**Impact.** What benefits will our stakeholders begin to see? Will their instructional practices improve? Will they see clarity in our school focus?

Once you work through the model from left to right, it's equally as important to go back and read from right to left. If your group wants to make the biggest possible impact, they need to decide how teachers and students will benefit, what steps to take, what activities to plan, and what resources will be needed. Teams must make sure that they have the needs solidly in place before moving forward.

Program logic encourages us to keep thinking big while we start focusing on the small components that will help us achieve our vision, which Fullan refers to as *nuance*. In his book *Nuance: Why Some Leaders Succeed and Others Fail*, Fullan wrote, "A key dimension of nuance is to be able to see the big picture—the *system*—while at the same time being able to understand the details and their connections and hidden patterns operating within the system itself" (2019, p. 3). Before starting any implementation, you need to get to the heart of the improvement, which of course should be based on the current reality of the school. It may take several team meetings to work out your goals.

////////////////////////////////////////////////////////////////////////////////

## Student Voice Questions

Looking at the program logic model, do you think this way of thinking could enhance student learning? How might the program logic model be used to help students understand why they are learning and what they are learning?

////////////////////////////////////////////////////////////////////////////////

Figure 2.3 is a more defined example of program logic to encourage big thinking around the important element of common language and common understanding among school staff members. It provides a very specific example of an issue that requires program logic before implementation cycles can occur.

In this much more defined example, we can see that the members of the leadership team realized at the *Needs* stage of the process that they had a common language around terms such as "growth mindset" and "student engagement," but they did not have a common understanding of the definitions of those terms.

In looking at the evidence they collected about their needs, they found that the principal believed that "student engagement" is authentic engagement where students are engaged in classroom discussion and focuses on strategies that help students speak up in the classroom, while several teachers believed "student engagement" is more about compliance, where they do the majority of the talking in the classroom.

The team then talked about the resources and activities needed to create the opportunity for outputs, which could involve flipped faculty meetings, or a flipped experience during professional learning community (PLC) and department meetings, as well as working with the principal to focus on common language and understanding during the walkthrough process.

The discussion a group has around the program logic model and what they need to implement is not a linear discussion. It is a conversation that needs to be revisited continually, which makes it a perfect topic for a monthly stakeholder meeting. It takes several planning meetings to go back and forth to make sure all the pieces agreed upon in the program logic model fit

Figure 2.3    Program Logic Model Example: Establishing Common Language and Common Understanding

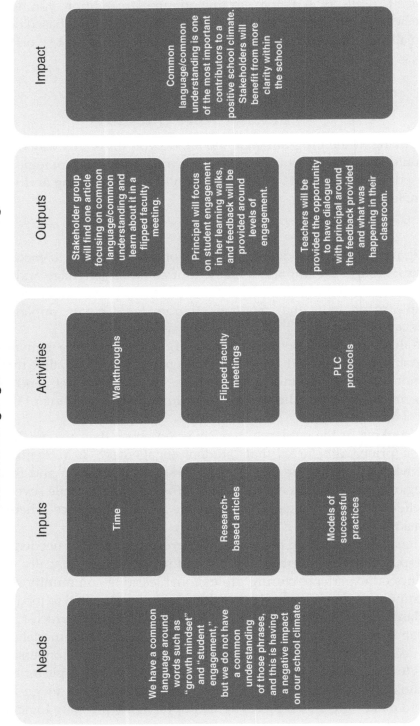

## Common Language/Common Understanding

**Needs**

We have a common language around words such as "growth mindset" and "student engagement," but we do not have a common understanding of those phrases, and this is having a negative impact on our school climate.

**Inputs**

Time

Research-based articles

Models of successful practices

**Activities**

Walkthroughs

Flipped faculty meetings

PLC protocols

**Outputs**

Stakeholder group will find one article focusing on common language/common understanding and learn about it in a flipped faculty meeting.

Principal will focus on student engagement in her learning walks, and feedback will be provided around levels of engagement.

Teachers will be provided the opportunity to have dialogue with principal around the feedback provided and what was happening in their classroom.

**Impact**

Common language/common understanding is one of the most important contributors to a positive school climate. Stakeholders will benefit from more clarity within the school.

together, and it takes multiple follow-up meetings to make sure the model created is working. Although Hargreaves and Fink were focusing on professional learning communities, their list of ideas fit perfectly with the process behind a successful program logic model when they stated that the following components are necessary to collaborative work (2006, p. 560):

- Modeling and building strong and rewarding relationships by paying attention to the human side of school change
- Establishing a high-trust environment
- Developing and renewing a culture of learning and improvement at all levels through problem solving, inquiry, and intelligent evidence-informed decision making
- Helping the school community develop and commit to a cohesive and compelling purpose that prevents dissipation of initiative and effort
- Stimulating a culture of professional entrepreneurship in innovations and ideas that benefit student learning
- Establishing and regulating grown-up professional norms of civil argument and productive debate
- Ensuring the voices of minority members of the culture always receive a proper hearing
- Doing all this within an unswerving commitment to improving all students' learning and achievement, especially for those who are furthest behind

The evolving nature of this process makes the program logic model a fluid document, because it may change based on the evidence the group is collecting. The evidence may show that the group needs to change or adjust an activity or that another input needs to be factored in that wasn't considered before.

As one last addition, I think it important to give a short list of dos and don'ts. Figure 2.4 is meant to help bring a little more clarity to the program logic process.

### Mindful Moment

We often have a common language and use terms such as "instructional leadership," "student engagement," "growth mindset," and "differentiated instruction," but we often lack a common understanding of those terms. We use the same words, but because we may not agree on the meaning behind them, we put our ideas into practice in very different ways.

Reflect on the language of learning in your school. How do you ensure that there is a common language and common understanding around learning?

**Figure 2.4**   Dos and Don'ts of Program Logic

| Do: | Don't: |
|---|---|
| • Create a program logic model with a group of diverse thinkers.<br>• Decide what your greatest area of improvement should be. What is your current reality? What impact would you like to see happen for the whole school community?<br>• Slow down the process of implementation by convening the group several times to make sure the program logic model is clear and concise. | • Create a program logic model in isolation.<br>• Create a program logic model to justify an activity. Instead, use a program logic model to help you decide what activity will have the greatest impact on student learning.<br>• Rush the process. Program logic models are all about inspiring deep and transfer thinking.<br>• Overload the program logic model with too many resources, activities, or outputs. |

After stakeholders go through the program logic model, it is time to move into the implementation cycle, focusing on just one of the activities agreed upon by the group. To highlight this whole process, let's concentrate on one example: walkthroughs.

## From Program Logic to Implementation Cycle

Program logic encourages us to focus on specific activities that will benefit the building community. In the example above, one of the activities that will help lead to a common language and common understanding is the walk-through process. Walkthroughs tend to be much more complicated than principals understand before they dive into doing them.

Instructional leadership practices, like walkthroughs, when implemented without deep thought and planning, can do more harm than good. When teachers see a feedback sheet, which is a popular strategy used in today's leadership practices, they do not necessarily think that the strategy is about growth. Many times they think the strategy is about building compliance, because too often principals never talk with teachers about their observations—they just complete walkthroughs. This creates a disconnect in the relationship between the teacher and principal, which can harm future learning opportunities. This is just one example of how leadership actions can disrupt a school community.

When leaders use the program logic model to create activities that will help them achieve an improvement, there needs to be a methodical approach to carrying out those activities, to ensure that successful implementation. With all of that being said, the following is an illustration of an implementation cycle focusing on walkthroughs, which acts as an extension of our earlier conversation around program logic.

**Figure 2.5** Implementation Strategy for Walkthroughs

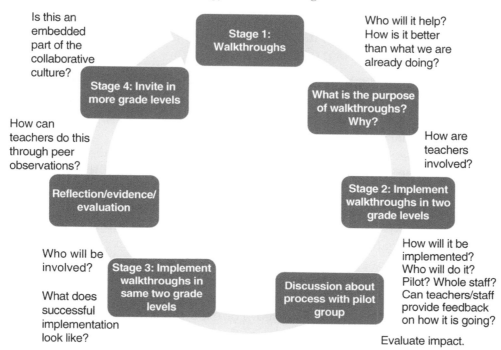

Based on research by Odom, Duda, Kucharczyk, Cox, & Stabel (2014) and Fixsen, Naoom, Blasé, Friedman, & Wallace (2005).

## IMPLEMENTATION MULTI-STAGE MODEL

*Stage 1: New practice to be implemented—what activity was chosen to help implement an improvement?* Creating and communicating a specific vision for the practice will provide leaders with the opportunity to be proactive. Odom et al. stated that "implementation, by necessity, requires a clearly articulated program model." This is part of stage 1, because teachers can ask questions and provide feedback about the strategy at its inception.

Who will it help?

How is it better than what we are already doing?

How will it be implemented?

Who will do it?

Pilot?

What is the end result?

What are the expectations of everyone where this strategy is concerned?

Teachers are not in the heads of their leaders, so leaders need to meet teachers where they are, model what the practice looks like and motivate teachers to be a part of it (DeWitt, 2016a).

*Stage 2: Actual implementation of walkthroughs.* This is where the rubber meets the road! The leader begins implementing the strategy. Perhaps the new strategy is focused on walkthroughs, and this is where the principal begins the formal walkthrough process.

*Reflection/evidence/evaluation discussion.* This is where teachers—whether it's the full staff, a PLC, or a group that is piloting the strategy—partner with the principal to provide feedback and offer suggestions for improvement. According to DiNapoli (2016), the core components of implementation science are dissemination of effectiveness research and successful integration of treatments and interventions at multiple levels. If we are to evaluate the implementation process and intervene effectively, we must collect evidence to gain an understanding of how successful the implementation is at this point, and everyone involved must be able to evaluate the impact of the improvement being implemented. For example, this is a point at which leaders and teachers relate examples of the feedback the principal gave and whether it helped them change practice.

*Stage 3: Second round of implementation of walkthroughs.* The principal begins the second phase of the implementation, taking into consideration the feedback from staff members. In our walkthrough example, this is where the principal might go back into the same classrooms from stage 2 and offer verbal feedback, not just written feedback as in the first stage.

*Reflection/evidence/evaluate discussion.* Now that teachers and their leader are beginning to get used to the process, teachers offer further feedback. The group makes adjustments to implementation based on the evaluations of the improvement thus far, and stakeholders keep discussing what a successful implementation might look like. Additionally, this is where evidence is discussed again, to see whether improvements have taken place after stages 1 and 2.

*Stage 4: Will this be embedded in collaborative culture?* Has the practice become embedded in the school culture yet? If not, why? If so, how do we move forward together? This is a very important stage, because it means the strategy being implemented has expanded to involve more of the staff, and it provides the opportunity for leaders to prove that this is not a passing phase.

*Reflection/evidence/evaluate discussion.* Now that all teachers and their leader are fully accustomed to the process, they have a clear discussion reflecting on implementation of the improvement for the whole school. Teachers offer further feedback; the group makes adjustments in implementation based on evaluation of the improvement thus far and then focuses on a successful implementation.

////////////////////////////////////////////////////////////////////////////////

## Student Voice Questions

How might you maintain a student focus when using the implementation cycle?

How often do students come up as the reason for an implementation?

////////////////////////////////////////////////////////////////////////////////

This cycle of implementation will continue to grow, and there may be more than four stages, depending on the activity being implemented. This also means that at the stakeholder meeting where program logic is discussed and evaluated, stakeholders need to talk about how each of the activities is helping meet the greater good. High-quality implementation means that leaders and stakeholders need to continue to go through a cycle until the evidence supports that they have reached their goal.

Figure 2.6

| Principals Advisory Council | |
| --- | --- |
| Pre-Reading | Read Peter DeWitt's blog post "The Myth of Walkthroughs" (see page 74). Two questions to ponder before the meeting:<br>1. Do our walkthroughs perpetuate this myth?<br>2. What is one suggestion you have to make our walkthroughs more impactful? |
| 3:00 – 3:15 | Discuss DeWitt's blog post. |
| 3:15 – 3:45 | Reflect on and evaluate our walkthrough process. |
| 3:45 – 4:15 | Revisit the program logic model. Questions to discuss:<br>1. Do we have a common language and common understanding? Provide examples.<br>2. Has it resulted in an increase in student engagement?<br>3. Are students using common language (i.e., vocabulary) and have a common understanding in their classes (i.e., science, math, etc.)? |

Additionally, at each stakeholder meeting, which in most schools happens once a month, each person involved in the walkthrough process will discuss how it is going. To end this chapter and put it all together, Figure 2.6 shows an example agenda for a stakeholder meeting.

## In the End

Leaders sometimes begin doing activities without any clear sense of why and how they are doing them. They get on social media and read about getting out of their offices and doing walkthroughs, so they quickly follow the recommendations and do that. Unfortunately, without the right thinking around why we are doing it, and without the dialogue that needs to happen with teachers whose classrooms are entered into, we begin to create a disconnected school climate rather than a connected one.

Program logic is an important first step in any improvement that leaders want to engage in. As you learned from the example provided in this chapter, a walkthrough is merely an activity to get a school community to center around a much more important focus: a common language and common understanding. Program logic is a process that may take several meetings, and it is important to include the voices of a diverse group of thinkers, usually referred to as a stakeholder group.

In summary, in order to achieve the necessary impact, an implementation cycle needs to be created for every activity that is chosen to support the agreed-upon goal. This illustrates the importance of our choice of each activity during the implementation process. That implementation cycle requires dialogue that involves feedback from everyone involved in the process, which is why I suggest beginning with a pilot group. That pilot group may be a fraction of the whole stakeholder group, but its members can offer important insight. Clearly, this is a lot of work, which is why leaders must collaborate and choose wisely when it comes to the activities.

## STUDY GUIDE QUESTIONS

- As a leadership group, what do you believe is the relationship between implementation and improvement?
- What are the biggest challenges that might arise as you go through the program logic process?
- What are some improvements needed in your school district or school board, and how could you use the program logic model to achieve that goal?

- How much time does your school district normally spend on implementation of a new program?
- In your building, how long do you spend on implementation? The answer will be "It depends," but do you feel that you spend enough time on implementation? Why or why not?
- As a leadership team, or in your own individual leadership practices, do your stakeholder meetings align with the improvement being implemented?
- As a group, can you make the effort to look past *change* in an effort to focus on *improvement*?

# 3

# A FOCUS ON LEARNING

## Deepening Our Impact as Instructional Leaders

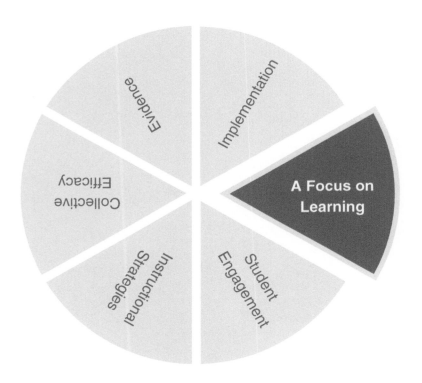

Scan this QR code for a video introduction to the chapter.

W hat should leaders be expected to know when they enter into classrooms or talk with teachers and students in the hallway? In many countries, leaders have always been asked to play the role of manager, in which they focus on the day-to-day functions of a school or concern themselves with budgets and parental engagement. In contrast, instructional leadership is when those in a leadership position focus on implementing practices that will increase student learning. Although instructional leadership has been heavily researched over the last 50 years, the idea of focusing on leadership practices that positively impact student learning is a fairly new one for some leaders. While research has focused on instructional leadership, many building principals have been focusing instead on management, which is an example of the disconnect between research and practice. The expectation that principals be instructional leaders is generating dialogue around exactly what role leaders should take in the teaching and learning that happen in school.

Defining the role of the leader when it comes to teaching and learning is a question I have been confronted with lately at conferences and in coaching sessions around the world, such as in the United Kingdom, Scandinavia, and Australia. I love to dive into different contexts and listen to the issues that building leaders, teacher leaders, and instructional coaches face in their particular educational system. What I have found is that many people believe that leaders should be expected to be content experts in every area. This idea of leaders being content experts piques my interest. Why is it that, in addition to all the tasks and responsibilities that leaders are charged with, they should be experts in every content area taught in an entire school building?

Advocates for content expertise are of the belief that the more leaders understand the content, the more impactful they will be as instructional leaders. As much as I can see why, the reality is that leaders have little time to get to know all the content taught by all the teachers of all the grade levels under their leadership. Leaders are so weighed down already, I worry this expectation of content expertise will place so much burden on them that they will leave the role. Therefore, in my opinion, being a content expert doesn't matter as much as asking teachers important questions about what students are learning in the classroom.

> Being a content expert doesn't matter as much as asking teachers important questions about what students are learning in the classroom.

## Mindful Moment

Take a moment to relax and breathe.

Ask yourself: What is the relationship between your leadership practices and what students learn? What do you believe you do during the day that impacts student learning in a positive way?

The debate about what leaders should be expected to know when it comes to student learning relates to a macro-level conversation about how our students should be educated and, specifically, what and how they should learn.

////////////////////////////////////////////////////////////////////////////

## Student Voice Questions

How often do you ask students how they learn? How often do your conversations with students include why students are learning what they are learning?

////////////////////////////////////////////////////////////////////////////

We never seem to look for the middle ground in all of this debate. Researchers and publishing houses believe their way is the best way, so we should buy what they are selling because it is what our students truly need. I believe we should look at all of the information and find a balance in it all. We need to find a balance between listening to outside expertise, on one hand, and focusing inward and listening to our staff, on the other. You must understand the current reality when it comes to student learning and decide how to go deeper in the practices that are already taking place in your school. Let's begin with a discussion of knowledge versus skills.

## TYPES OF LEARNING: KNOWLEDGE VS. SKILLS

Our students need a balance between knowledge and skills. Knowledge is important, but being able to process information or complicated learning situations both academically and social-emotionally requires skills as well. Figure 3.1 may help illustrate the difference between the two more clearly.

As you can see, knowledge is about understanding facts and concepts. Both are extremely important to the learning process. As leaders, when we enter into classrooms or have educational conversations with parents, students or teachers, we need to develop an understanding of which classrooms focus on both factual and conceptual knowledge and which ones really focus on one more than the other. As we know, facts are important, but it is equally as important that our students understand how learning can become interrelated and dependent on itself. This knowledge aligns with conceptual understanding.

The other side of Erickson's example focuses on process. What strategies can we give our students in order to cope, and what skills do students need to understand how to achieve their own learning? If leaders are going to

**Figure 3.1**   Erickson's Knowledge vs. Process

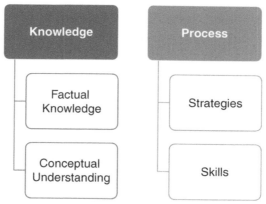

Adapted from Erickson, H. L. (2008).

begin having walkthroughs and formal observations with depth, they need to begin thinking about the different types of learning that are taking place in classrooms. They also need to understand which classrooms focus on one area of learning, such as factual knowledge, more than on another, such as conceptual knowledge. Identifying the type of learning that is occurring in each classroom allows leaders to have more of a keen eye in those informal and formal observation situations, and it also allows them to have more robust conversations with teachers, students, and families. Another facet of learning that leaders need to understand in order to deepen their practice is the topic of surface-, deep-, and transfer-level learning.

////////////////////////////////////////////////////////////////

## Student Voice Questions

Do students who major in career technical education (CTE) understand that you respect them as much as those students who major in liberal arts, math and science, or the arts?

////////////////////////////////////////////////////////////////

## LEVELS OF LEARNING: SURFACE, DEEP, AND TRANSFER

Understanding and identifying the levels of learning that are happening in the classroom is a very important aspect of instructional leadership. Our time is much better spent when we can take our walkthroughs, engage in faculty meetings and conversations with teachers, and align them so that we can better understand what is going on in classrooms within our schools.

Instead of always focusing on standards, I believe we should focus on creating dialogue with teachers and students around evidence of impact and how students' learning will help them both now and in their future. I'm tired of hearing people say that students need to know information because it's on a test. That's a political answer, and it's one that seldom focuses on good learning. Let's start having fewer political answers and begin fostering better pedagogical ones.

*Surface-level* understanding comes when learning is brand-new for students. For example, when we're teaching teenagers to drive a car, we keep our instructions and lessons very simple so as not to overwhelm the new driver. We first have to teach the students some mechanical basics, like where the brake and gas pedals are, and where the fuel goes. We can then slowly connect the actual in-car experience to each student's prior knowledge, such as from a classroom-based driver's-ed course. We then help students learn how delicately or firmly they need to turn the steering wheel of the particular car they are driving. We guide them through all the preliminary questions that will become second nature after some driving experience (e.g., Are the mirrors all adjusted properly before getting underway?). Then, we allow them to cruise slowly in a safe area, such as an empty parking lot. As they put what they have learned into practice, we give simple cues, gauging their level of understanding, and providing quick one-step directions (e.g., "Brake!") to guide their learning.

We need to have that same mindset when we enter classrooms to observe learning in action. How are teachers creating a safe environment for students? Are they giving them some basic instructions around the learning (i.e., the rules of the road) and connecting it to students' prior knowledge?

Not to complicate the situation, but every time we discuss how we are helping students understand new learning, we need to couple that with asking teachers how they are scaffolding the information to ensure that students who already possess a higher level of understanding are challenged as well. Surface-, deep-, and transfer-level learning may come quickly to one student, but with dozens of students to a class, it may be a little more messy because the whole class does not always achieve the same level of understanding at the same time.

*Deep-level learning* comes after students have had some experience with the content being learned. They need to activate that prior knowledge to get to a deeper level. That's where we move from the slow drive around the parking lot to taking the car on some of the main roads in town. We begin to ask our new drivers "What if" questions, like "What if we hear an ambulance coming up quickly behind us when we are driving? What should we do?" It's when teachers should be using organizational strategies or concept mapping with students, so that those students can begin to mind-map the challenges that accompany the new learning.

When leaders enter classrooms and see this type of teaching and learning taking place, they can begin to ask students about the intentions of the lesson and ensure that those intentions will lead to deep-level learning for those students. When leaders sit down with students and ask them what they are learning, students should be able to articulate the learning and not just the activity that may be the vehicle for the learning.

Lastly, *transfer-level learning* builds on the surface and deep learning that came prior. We all need to find effective methods of helping students get to the deep and transfer levels of learning, because we often spend too much time on surface level. Transfer level is when students can "hit the highway" with all of that prior driving knowledge and put it to use by beginning to drive in complicated areas on their own. It is about understanding multiple directions at the same time the learning gets a bit more complicated, and applying that learning in other parts of their lives.

> ### Mindful Moment
>
> Take a moment to put this learning into your context as a leader. Surface-, deep-, and transfer-level learning isn't just the job of a teacher. This progression of learning needs to take place among other adults as well. Our formal professional learning and development, faculty meetings, and PLC meetings should provide the opportunity for teachers to go from surface, to deep, to transfer learning.

**Example** – In Chapter 2, I used the program logic model to show how a school leadership team might focus on common language and common understanding around the term "student engagement." To continue with the same topic, here are three quick ways to get faculty from surface- to deep- to transfer-level learning with the concept of student engagement.

- **Surface**—Teachers read an article focusing on student engagement techniques.
- **Deep**—Teachers bring evidence of a student engagement strategy they use in the classroom and share their best practice.
- **Transfer**—Teachers take one peer-shared idea and try the technique in the classroom, where leaders may see it in action during walkthroughs. Teachers can bring evidence of how it worked to the next scheduled faculty meeting.

Figure 3.2 draws on the work of Hattie and Donoghue (2016), who listed instructional strategies that will help students acquire surface-level learning and then consolidate that learning; acquire deep-level learning and then consolidate that deep level of understanding; and, finally, look for similarities

**Figure 3.2**   Surface- to Deep- Learning Strategies

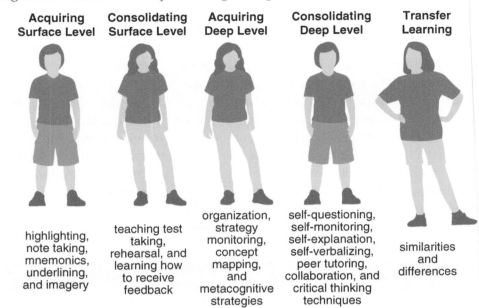

| Acquiring Surface Level | Consolidating Surface Level | Acquiring Deep Level | Consolidating Deep Level | Transfer Learning |
|---|---|---|---|---|
| highlighting, note taking, mnemonics, underlining, and imagery | teaching test taking, rehearsal, and learning how to receive feedback | organization, strategy monitoring, concept mapping, and metacognitive strategies | self-questioning, self-monitoring, self-explanation, self-verbalizing, peer tutoring, collaboration, and critical thinking techniques | similarities and differences |

*Source of Graphics:* iStock.com/rangepuppies.

and differences between what they have learned throughout the first two levels of learning. In multiple subject areas.

## Student Voice Questions

How often are the learning strategies represented in Figure 3.2 explicitly taught in your school? How often do students have the opportunity to talk about which strategies work best for them?

One specific strategy that can help promote the surface, deep, and transfer learning that Hattie and Donoghue discuss is the use of graphic organizers. The Australian Society for Evidence Based Teaching (n.d.) suggests that teachers can use common graphic organizers, such as the following, to help students visualize the mental processes involved in learning.

- **Linking to Prior Knowledge** (use progressive mind-maps, cumulative concept maps and KLR charts—what do I already **know**, what have I **learned**, how does this **relate** to what I knew)
- **Hierarchical Classification** (use mind-maps, t-charts, e-charts, fishbone charts and tree diagrams)

- **Cause-Effect** (use cause-effect chains, trees and webs)
- **Comparison** (use Venn diagrams, tables, continuums)
- **Sequence** (use timelines, sequence charts and cycle diagrams)
- **Drawing Conclusions** (use LUC charts and multi-flow maps)

As instructional leaders, we need to know what to look for in classrooms and what to try to stimulate dialogue about in our PLC, grade-level, department, and faculty meetings. When discussing and debating surface, deep, and transfer learning, the Australian Society for Evidence Based Teaching (n.d.) offers these eight tips for deep learning:

## 8 Tips for Deep Learning

1. Explicitly teach students the knowledge that they need to think about topics more deeply.
2. Once students have sufficient knowledge, set lesson goals focused on deep learning.
3. Model and let students practice deep-learning strategies before asking them to do so independently.
4. Teach students how to use graphic organizers to show relationships and to nurture deeper thinking.
5. Have students apply thinking strategies to content they have learned.
6. Assess students' thinking.
7. Give students feedback about misconceptions they hold (faulty thinking) and about the depth of thought that their work reflects.
8. Incidentally use deep learning strategies yourself throughout the day, and use *think-alouds* to model this practice for your students.

---

### Mindful Moment

Reflect a bit here. What do you look for when you go into classrooms? Do you look for student work? Or do you prefer professionally made or teacher-made charts that help students move forward when they are stuck? Do you talk with students when you are in the classroom?

---

## KNOWLEDGE DIMENSIONS

Our instructional leadership practices also need to align with an understanding of and focus on knowledge dimensions. There are four knowledge dimensions in the cognitive process (Anderson & Krathwohl 2001b, Stern,

Lauriault, & Ferraro, 2018): factual knowledge, conceptual knowledge, procedural knowledge, and metacognitive knowledge. Within each of these knowledge dimensions, teachers and students can go from surface- to deep- and then on to transfer-level learning.

Anderson and Krathwohl adapted the knowledge dimensions from Bloom's Taxonomy, and the dimensions are specifically designed to be viewed as learning objectives and not learning activities. Knowledge dimensions are not only the catalyst for a conversation around engagement and instructional strategies (Chapters 4–5), but they are also necessary when we think of how we can offer our students a well-rounded education. We cannot dive into understanding robust instructional strategies or academic and social-emotional student engagement without highlighting and diving into knowledge dimensions. Many schools focus on Depths of Knowledge (DOK) or SOLO taxonomy, and they should continue with that focus if they share a common language and common understanding within those frameworks with their teachers. However, many leaders that I work with do not have a framework to draw from when they engage in walkthroughs or observations, and the knowledge dimensions are a very solid place to begin.

In our daily practices, knowledge dimensions are the core objectives of the learning taking place in the classroom, and they provide us with a perfect topic to discuss in our instructional leadership practices. We can focus on these four dimensions during faculty and department meetings, as well as grade-level meetings, formal teacher observations and informal conversations with teachers, other staff members and instructional coaches.

Figure 3.3 provides definitions of each knowledge dimension (Anderson & Krathwohl, 2001b; Stern et al., 2018). For instructional leadership to occur, we need to take this knowledge of the four dimensions and think of ways to begin using it.

Beginning with *factual knowledge*, we can see that this is often the type of learning schools have been known to promote over the years. Factual knowledge is the knowledge of details and isolated bits of information. Factual knowledge involves the basic elements a student must know within a discipline and in order to solve problems within that discipline. If you have ever taught literacy, you know that general vocabulary can play a large role in the acquisition of language, which is important to the literacy rates of our students. In a similar way, specific vocabularies are quite important to science, social studies, math, music and virtually every content area offered in schools. In order to get by, you first have to know the lingo. This composes factual knowledge.

**Figure 3.3**    The Four Knowledge Dimensions

| Knowledge Dimension | |
|---|---|
| Factual | Factual knowledge includes isolated bits of information, such as vocabulary definitions and knowledge about specific details. |
| Conceptual | Conceptual knowledge consists of systems of information, such as classifications and categories. |
| Procedural | Procedural knowledge involves knowledge of skills, such as how to carry out a task. |
| Metacognitive | Metacognitive knowledge refers to knowledge of thinking processes and information about how to manipulate these processes effectively. |

Adapted from Anderson & Krathwohl (2001a, b) and Stern et al. (2018).

As far as details are concerned, we know that understanding details helps us process information, which leads to procedural knowledge. Dates and timelines help us compose plots and settings, as well as understand when history took place.

Understanding the role that factual knowledge plays in education is important. Factual knowledge can help lay the foundation for all other learning. However, what we also have to understand is that, at some point, teachers need to move on from just teaching factual knowledge and move on to a deeper level of learning, which moves us into *conceptual knowledge.*

Conceptual knowledge provides a journey toward deep-level learning by looking at those interrelationships within our learning. After they understand facts and details, students can use that knowledge to begin seeing patterns across their larger world. It's often something adults in school take for granted because it has become automatic for us. Conceptual understanding helps students see, for example, how they can take those timelines and settings and begin to understand what was happening at the same time in history in another country.

*Procedural knowledge* is the knowledge of skills. In our teenage-drivers example, the students gain important procedural knowledge as they learn the mechanics of a car so that they can troubleshoot and repair the car on their own. In the classroom, students gain procedural knowledge as they learn how to solve equations in math, as they build phonemic awareness to develop their reading skills, or as they master the basics of the scientific method to develop an investigation and make breakthroughs in science. It's a short road from factual knowledge to procedural knowledge, but here's the difference. As we know, facts remain fairly constant. However, when developing skills for reading, the process may change as students increasingly read and sound out larger words, which means that procedural knowledge can transfer to allow for deeper understandings as the learning gets more complex.

Lastly, there is *metacognitive knowledge*, which is the ultimate in deep and transfer-level learning. It means that students are at a point in their learning where they understand their way of thinking, how they got to where they are, and where they can take themselves next. This overall awareness that students have of their own learning is built through self-monitoring and self-verbalization, as well as peer tutoring.

To further illustrate each of the knowledge dimensions, Figure 3.4 gives some simple examples of each.

As in other chapters throughout the book, I want to provide you with a program logic view—in this case, of implementing knowledge dimensions in your school, in the event that it may be useful. Keep in mind that this program logic model is meant to be an example. Leaders may find that this example provides them with a starting point, but they can develop something more robust or effective for their own contexts.

**Figure 3.4**   Examples of Each Knowledge Dimension

| Factual | When was JFK assassinated? What are some of the reasons that contributed to the Vietnam War? What does a .40 effect size mean in Hattie's research? |
| --- | --- |
| Conceptual | What is the relationship between *Harry Potter and the Sorcerer's Stone* by J. K. Rowling and *The Hobbit* by J. R. R. Tolkien? What is the relationship between the research around school leadership and what you experience in your school? |
| Procedural | What is the order of operations? How would you go about sounding out that first word in the sentence? |
| Metacognitive | What did you learn today that challenged your thinking? |

Figure 3.5    Program Logic Model Example: Knowledge Dimensions

**Knowledge Dimensions**

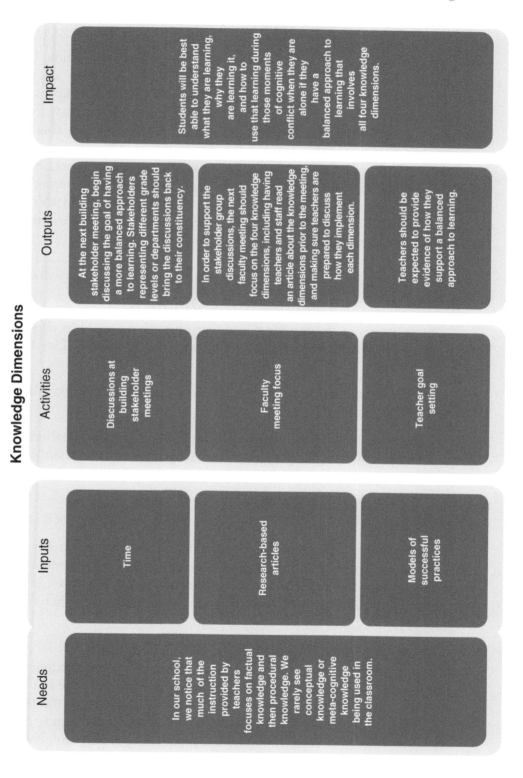

| Needs | Inputs | Activities | Outputs | Impact |
|---|---|---|---|---|
| In our school, we notice that much of the instruction provided by teachers focuses on factual knowledge and then procedural knowledge. We rarely see conceptual knowledge or meta-cognitive knowledge being used in the classroom. | Time | Discussions at building stakeholder meetings | At the next building stakeholder meeting, begin discussing the goal of having a more balanced approach to learning. Stakeholders representing different grade levels or departments should bring the discussions back to their constituency. | Students will be best able to understand what they are learning, why they are learning it, and how to use that learning during those moments of cognitive conflict when they are alone if they have a balanced approach to learning that involves all four knowledge dimensions. |
| | Research-based articles | Faculty meeting focus | In order to support the stakeholder group discussions, the next faculty meeting should focus on the four knowledge dimensions, including having teachers and staff read an article about the knowledge dimensions prior to the meeting, and making sure teachers are prepared to discuss how they implement each dimension. | |
| | Models of successful practices | Teacher goal setting | Teachers should be expected to provide evidence of how they support a balanced approach to learning. | |

## In the End

What used to be a separation between teachers and leaders has now become a place to bond those two groups together. Leaders need to know how learning works, and the focus behind learning, in order to improve their walkthroughs, observations, and discussions in those places that focus on learning. Leaders who lack that background knowledge are less able to give teachers effective feedback.

From a very practical sense, having an understanding of knowledge dimensions and the types of learning that take place in classrooms allows leaders to be more integral when creating a school climate that focuses on learning. In addition, it helps them understand how to involve parents in their children's learning.

////////////////////////////////////////////////////////////////////////

## Student Voice Questions

How much of the teaching and learning taking place in classrooms focuses on one knowledge dimension over the rest? Do students know this?

Is there balance among the types of learning taking place for students?

Which students in the classroom can answer factual knowledge, but lack the ability to display more metacognitive development because they do not get the opportunity to be introduced to that type of learning?

As leaders, how can we help teachers and students in all of this?

Can we work with teachers in our faculty meetings around a sample focus on learning and decide which knowledge dimensions will help achieve that learning? Can students be encouraged to provide a short presentation about what each knowledge dimension might look like?

////////////////////////////////////////////////////////////////////////

When entering classrooms or talking with teachers and students about learning, we need to make sure that there is a balance among the knowledge dimensions, which will depend on where the students are in the learning process. For example, when students are just beginning to learn new content, factual knowledge will most likely be the focus. As a leader involved with doing walkthroughs or formal conversations with teachers, it's important that you ask, and understand, what the learning objectives are behind a lesson, and whether the learning objectives or goals focus disproportionately on factual knowledge.

There is so much good in all of this information, and it begins with understanding the four knowledge dimensions. We need to combine how students learn with what students learn, and follow up by discussing the best ways to engage students in that learning. Our moral obligation is to inspire students to think for themselves, and our actions in the classroom may not always provide that inspiration if we have low expectations of students.

Instructional leadership is about working with teachers to combine our thinking and talk about the necessary elements of challenge for students. Instructional leaders need to understand focus on learning more than they need to have content expertise. State academic standards may change, but looking for student engagement and high-quality instruction will never change. I believe we can do a better job of helping students go from surface- to deep- to transfer-level learning using better instructional strategies, which I will cover in the next chapter. One of the ways we can encourage this shift is by being instructional leaders who know what to look for in our everyday practices.

> Instructional leaders need to understand focus for learning more than they need to have content expertise.

## STUDY GUIDE QUESTIONS

- As a leadership team, what conversations around knowledge versus skills do you have in your schools?
- What knowledge and skills would you hope that the average student from your school possesses by the time he or she graduates?
- How are you helping promote those hoped-for outcomes right now?
- What examples of surface-, deep-, and transfer-level learning do you see taking place in classrooms?
- As a leadership team, if you did an instructional round together, do you believe you would see one type of learning emphasized over the rest? Or would you see balance among them all?
- As leaders, how do you provide professional learning opportunities for teachers where they experience surface-, deep- and transfer-level learning?
- How often do you talk with teachers about the four knowledge dimensions?
- Just as with surface-, deep- and transfer-level learning, does a particular knowledge dimension seem to dominate in your school? Or, if your team did an instructional round together, would you see a balanced approach?
- Provide some specific examples of how you look for the four knowledge dimensions in your walkthroughs.

# STUDENT ENGAGEMENT

## From Alienation to Social-Emotional Learning

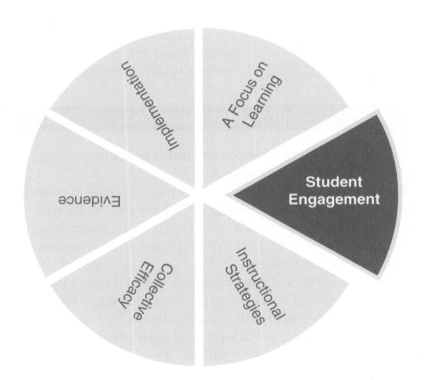

Scan this QR code for a video introduction to the chapter.

As we know, "student engagement" is a very broad term, because it encompasses so much when we think about our schools. "Student engagement" refers to how our students feel supported when they enter our doors, and how they feel challenged by what we teach. It means that we know their names when they attend our classes, and it means we encourage them to take a risk and try out for a team sport, band or chorus, or the drama club.

Earlier in the book, I used the term "student engagement" as an example to highlight our need for a common language and a common understanding of the phrases and words we so often use in our schools. In the pursuit of common language and common understanding, let's begin with a working definition of *student engagement*.

Trowler (2010) defines student engagement as "the interaction between the time, effort and other relevant resources invested by both students and their institutions intended to optimise the student experience and enhance the learning outcomes and development of students and the performance, and reputation of the institution" (p. 3). Although Trowler focuses on higher education, the components of this definition fit into our K–12 needs as well.

### Mindful Moment

Reflect here for a moment. I have included student engagement in a few different areas of the book thus far. What comes to mind for you when you think of student engagement?

Trowler further defines the different components of student engagement, which got its start in the term "student involvement" back in the '80s. However, Trowler suggests that use of the term "student engagement" is primarily still confined to the United States, Canada, and Australia, whereas educators in the United Kingdom are more likely to use the terms "student feedback, student representation, student approaches to learning, institutional organisation, learning spaces, architectural design, and learning development" (2010, p. 2). This is important to understand, because as instructional leaders are always looking for resources to help us, we need to understand some of the different terms in order to help us find the best resources.

To further illustrate the discussion of student engagement, it's important to understand that there are numerous ways to look at the topic. Fredricks, Blumenfeld, and Paris (2004), with the aid of research by Bloom (1956), have divided student engagement into three dimensions: behavioral engagement, emotional engagement, and cognitive engagement. Coates (2009) measured student engagement along six scales. Those six scales are "academic challenge, active learning, student and staff interactions, enriching educational experiences, supportive learning environment, and work-integrated learning" (p. 6).

Figure 4.1 helps bring all of these definitions together so that we can focus on their universal themes.

As you can see, there is a great deal of crossover, which makes sense because all of the research focuses on engaging students. If we take this information and combine it with what we have learned regarding knowledge dimensions, we will find that there are really two umbrellas that all of this falls under, and those are social-emotional learning and academic learning.

In this chapter, we will explore social-emotional learning and what we can do as instructional leaders to try to engage students. This whole chapter will be devoted to the topic of social-emotional learning, because it plays such an important role in student engagement. We will focus on the academic aspect of student engagement in Chapter 5, when we explore instructional strategies. This will give us time to slow down the process of student engagement and couple it with

**Figure 4.1**    Definitions of Student Engagement

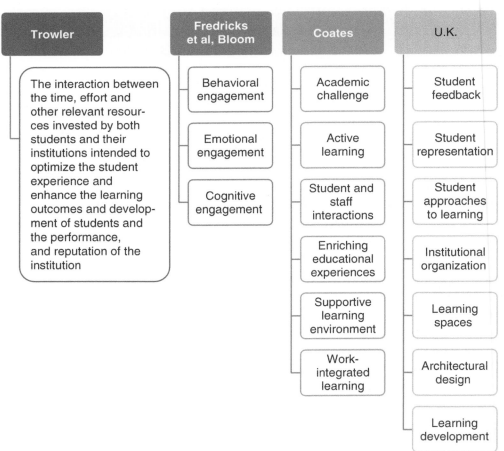

its necessary components. Social-emotional learning and academic learning are equally important when we are trying to engage our students.

Ultimately, this will help meet the goal of taking a whole-child approach, which means fostering academic and social-emotional growth in our students. Instructional leadership is about doing this for all of our students—and, yes, I'm aware that it is not an easy task.

Fostering a whole-child approach may reduce the number of students who feel alienated by our schools and help them meet their full potential. A whole-child approach means focusing on the social-emotional, as well as the academic, needs of our students.

## ALIENATION

Many times, instructional leadership is about looking for the "why" in each situation. Why is it important to focus on social-emotional learning? You may already understand the importance, or perhaps you aren't so sure. In fact, when I explore social-emotional learning in my *Finding Common Ground* blog for *Education Week,* I get a great deal of pushback from non-educators and educators alike. Sometimes I am surprised at how much pushback some topics bring, but out of all the topics I write about I get the most pushback when I focus on social-emotional learning. The critics do not believe that social-emotional learning belongs in our schools. I keep blogging about it anyway, because this is an important topic, and not all of our students come to school prepared mentally and physically for their day.

**Figure 4.2** Fostering a Whole-Child Approach to Learning

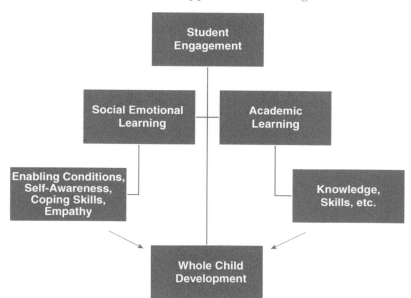

What we know is that we have many students suffering from trauma and mental health issues. Others come from unimaginably difficult home lives. Everything that students experience outside of school has an impact on how they learn. Some of our less fortunate students may begin to feel alienated within our school community because they do not feel as though they fit in. It is not as difficult as you might think for us to do a better job of meeting the needs of students who feel alienated, and we will explore this topic during both the social-emotional and academic sections in this chapter.

Mau (1989) found that alienation is attributable to several factors, which include "meritocratic grading system; curriculum tracking; the composition of students in neighbourhood schools; and student relationships with teachers and peers" (p. 17). I believe that alienation has recently worsened due to the pressure of high-stakes testing, because those students who do not score as well on tests feel devalued by some teachers and leaders. They know that they are being compared to students who helped their school look good when test scores were printed in the newspapers or posted online.

Mau explained the importance of teachers' actions in regard to the amount of alienation their students feel. "As agents of the school system, teachers influence the meritocratic achievement hierarchy by distributing more scarce rewards or higher grades to some students than others. Students with good grades feel greater efficacy and have better self-esteem than students with poor grades. In addition, students who meet teacher expectations may feel less alienation in the classroom" (1989, p. 21). We can infer from this that if teachers and leaders strive to have appropriate expectations of each student and downplay differences between them, it might reduce alienation. If teachers, for example, sometimes contribute to the problem of alienation because of biases toward specific students, they can also be part of the solution, by acknowledging those possible biases and learning to address them.

////////////////////////////////////////////////////////////////////

## Student Voice Questions

What avenues can students take in your school when they feel alienated because of a fractured relationship with a teacher or when they do not feel like they have a voice in their own learning? What supports are in place for them when they feel devalued? Are their voices respected when they speak of being devalued?

////////////////////////////////////////////////////////////////////

Odetola, Erickson, Bryan, and Walker (1972) found that there are two types of alienation that students feel within our schools, which the authors categorized as *identification* and *powerlessness*. Identification is defined as "the students' sense of belonging to his school" (p. 19). Powerlessness is a "students' feeling of incapacity to affect the direction of his learning" (p. 20). From a social-emotional learning stance, we have students who feel alienated because they feel marginalized. Marginalized populations feel excluded from the dialogue happening at their school, and they often feel as though their teachers have low expectations of them or do not care as much about them because they aren't a part of the dominant group, which is often heterosexual white students.

For example, many African American, LGBTQ, and indigenous students may feel alienated because the curriculum, the imagery and the dialogue in the school don't reflect their cultural background or sexual orientation. They perceive themselves as constantly missing from the "narrative" within their school when it fails to uphold the diversity of the student body. In order for these students to feel engaged, and less alienated, they need to have an emotional connection to their school community, and that is where social-emotional learning comes into play.

## SOCIAL-EMOTIONAL LEARNING

According to a 2018 study by the National Association of Elementary School Principals (Fuller, Young, Richardson, Pendola, & Winn, 2018, p. 33), over 80% of principals reported seeing an increase in the percentage of student mental health issues. This very statistic illustrates why instructional leadership is so complicated. It's difficult for leaders to focus on instructional leadership when they find themselves spending so much time helping students who are experiencing mental health issues.

To further illustrate all of this, let's add a few more statistics to show how much our school populations are changing. According to a report by the National Center for Children in Poverty in the United States (Bartlett, Smith, & Bringewatt, 2017), almost 35 million children in the United States (approximately 48%) have been exposed to one or more types of trauma, and young children are at disproportionate risk compared to older children (p. 4). In the United Kingdom, a report from King's College London found that one in four young people exposed to trauma met the criteria for PTSD, symptoms of which may include re-living traumatic events through distressing memories or nightmares; avoidance of anything reminding them of their trauma; feelings of guilt, isolation or detachment; and irritability, impulsivity or difficulty concentrating.

Research shows that students can experience trauma not only from catastrophic events but also as a result of prolonged stress in family situations, such as a divorce or a parent's mental health issues, and many students also have parents who need support. According to Tobin (2016):

Research in psychology and education suggests that trauma is associated with poorer education outcomes, and that traumatised children use more school and system-level academic supports, have lower academic achievement, and have higher rates of grade repetition and school drop-out.

The impact of poverty is equally as alarming. According to a report by the National Center for Children in Poverty (Koball & Jiang, 2018), among all children under 18 years in the United States, 41% are low-income children and 19%—approximately one in five—are poor. This means that children are overrepresented among our nation's poor; they represent 23% of the population but comprise 32% of all people in poverty.

The United States is not the only industrial nation with this sort of problem. According to the Social Metrics Commission (SMC), a UK organization, "there are as many as 4.5 million children [in the United Kingdom] currently living in poverty—a figure that accounts for 33 percent of the country's children. In the average class of 30 students, nine will be living in poverty" (2018, p. 7).

In Australia, the situation does not seem quite as bad, with "one in seven Australian children and young people living below the poverty line" (Smith Family, 2018). However, a low-income background is a serious handicap. "One in three children from disadvantaged backgrounds start school already behind and by age 15, the education gap is equivalent to three years of schooling" (Smith Family, 2018).

Ratcliffe (2015) found, in the United States, "Children who are poor are less likely to achieve important adult milestones, such as graduating from high school and enrolling in and completing college, than children who are never poor. For example, although more than 9 in 10 never-poor children (92.7 percent) complete high school, only 3 in 4 ever-poor children (77.9 percent) do so."

Social and emotional learning (SEL) is defined as "acquiring and effectively applying the knowledge, attitudes, and skills to understand and manage emotions, set and achieve positive goals, feel and show empathy for others, establish and maintain positive relationships, and make responsible decisions" (CASEL, 2013a, 2013b; Weissberg & Cascarino, 2013, p. 10). Trauma and poverty, which are big threats to social-emotional health, are not just a US issue—they're an international epidemic that we can all do something about.

---

### Mindful Moment

How has poverty or trauma impacted your ability to be an instructional leader?

In this chapter, I focus on some enabling conditions. This may help you find a balance between working through social-emotional stress and focusing on teaching and learning at the same time.

From the outside, it's easy to say that schools should focus only on learning, because the social-emotional issues that students face and how they play out at school are often invisible to the public. There are teachers who believe that SEL is the job of a counselor or school psychologist, not a teacher. In a similar vein, there are families who do not want schools to infringe on the beliefs they have at home.

In a book club focusing on my *School Climate: Leading With Collective Efficacy* (DeWitt, 2017), one principal told me that she thought social-emotional learning was important but got pushback from parents who wanted the school to focus more intently on AP courses, in order to get graduates into the "right" universities. We need not look to the recent college-admissions scandal to understand the pressures parents can place on schools to get their children into the right universities. And, too often, politicians cite the need to improve test scores as a reason for not focusing on SEL. But it's very difficult for students suffering from trauma to be fully engaged in academics if they are not supported socially and emotionally. Part of that involves teaching them how to deal with the stress they feel on a daily basis.

"Stress," according to Claxton (2007), "occurs when the Demands on a system significantly and persistently exceed the Resources which the system has to respond. If the Resources that people have at their disposal do not increase to meet an increase in the Demands they are experiencing, their attempts to cope may become increasingly desperate and dysfunctional" (p. 117).

Too often, though, teachers and leaders prioritize social-emotional learning only as a means of helping students who are dealing with trauma or mental health issues. There were many times that I was guilty of the same thing. I jumped on my soapbox and told everyone SEL was an area of need because we had so many students who were struggling. Then, my friend Marie-France Crête, an educator in Canada, reminded me that social-emotional learning is not just for students who struggle. All students benefit from learning how to collaborate, to have empathy for others, and to empower themselves when life gets tough. In fact, Crête wrote, "The sooner kids develop those skills, the better they do in school and the better the school climate will be" (personal communication, July 24, 2019). Social-emotional learning is not merely for those who are in devastating situations.

> Social-emotional learning is not merely for those who are in devastating situations.

All of this means that the question is not whether schools should be responsible for the social-emotional learning of their students. The question is how leaders can confront the social-emotional issues their students are facing while also devoting enough time to instructional leadership.

**Mindful Moment**

Reflect on your perspective on social-emotional learning. How do you focus on SEL with teachers in a way that moves beyond trauma and mental health to include all students?

## FIVE EASY STEPS TO SOCIAL-EMOTIONAL LEARNING

Meeting students' social-emotional needs does not have to be difficult. There are ways to meet a student's needs every day, and some of it is as simple as standing in the doorway. Following are five ways teachers and school leaders can truly embrace social-emotional learning to set examples for their communities:

1. **Greet students at the entrance—every single day.** This sounds like common sense, but let me provide some research to back up this example. According to the Quaglia Institute for School Voice and Aspirations (Quaglia, 2016), out of more than 100,000 students, only 52% believed their teachers took time to get to know them. Learning students' names and seeing them for who they are as individuals is the first and most important step toward a healthier classroom environment. And this advice doesn't extend only to teachers. It's equally as important for leaders to get to know students, so that they can "put faces on the data." When I myself was a school principal, I used to study the yearbook from the year before and attempt to memorize the names of students. Maybe you can try a similar means of familiarization.

2. **Use a high-quality social-emotional-learning curriculum.** An organized SEL curriculum can help teachers bring difficult or traumatic topics to light with students. Teachers might, for example, delve into the multitude of children's books and YA novels that explore situations or behavioral issues students are dealing with, which they can then weave seamlessly into academic learning. Try to be a leader to whom teachers can look for support in incorporating a social-emotional curriculum. Too many teachers worry that their principal is all about the academic side of learning, so leaders who support an SEL curriculum can help teachers feel more comfortable using it in their classrooms. The Collaborative for Social Emotional Learning (CASEL; https://casel.org) offers resources around resiliency and self-regulation.

3. **Hire more counselors and nurses.** Many schools lack the appropriate number of counselors and nurses to help students process their thoughts and feelings. Less than half of public schools in the United States employ a full-time nurse, and 21% of high schools don't have access to a school counselor. School leaders should advocate for more health professionals in schools to help meet the needs of students suffering from trauma and reduce the burden for counselors and nurses already on staff.

4. **Offer training for teachers.** Awareness is key. In order to support SEL, school and district leaders need to offer training to teachers on how to work with students in need. The organization or people doing the training should be carefully chosen to possess not only a deep understanding of SEL but also the added complexities of teaching. In addition, instructional leadership is about being in the room yourself during training. Doing so shows your support of the curriculum and allows you to learn new techniques to use with students as well.

5. **Improve the way you interact with students.** It sounds simple, but it can be hard to alter your habits. Small changes can make a big difference, however. For example, sometimes the very language that leaders use can have a positive or negative impact on students. When it comes to students who are at risk of alienation, you may be unable to improve their home environments, but you can certainly make them feel welcome in the school community. The chart below offers some suggestions for changing your dialogue with students. There is even space for you to add a few of your own ideas.

////////////////////////////////////////////////////////////////////////////

## Student Voice Questions

Stretch your thinking around the five steps above. In what ways do you make sure that students feel welcome and valued in your school?

////////////////////////////////////////////////////////////////////////////

**Mindful Moment**

Reflect on the transformations represented in Figure 4.3. While these "better" behaviors may seem like common sense, we often get busy in our daily lives as leaders and do not always react appropriately. Think about what you might add to this list. Then take a mental step back and reflect on a negative interaction you recently had with a student. If you could do things over again, how might you turn that interaction into a more positive one? Remember this the next time you're in a similar situation.

**Figure 4.3**   Suggestions for Improving Your Interactions With Students to Enhance SEL

| Instead of... | Try... |
| --- | --- |
| saying, "What did you do wrong?" | saying, "Tell me what happened." |
| just teaching content, | teaching children. |
| stopping students in the hallway and asking for a pass, | stopping students in the hallway and asking how their day is going. |
| focusing solely on academics, | focusing on social-emotional learning, too. |
| focusing on disciplining a problem, | focusing on getting to the heart of the issue. |
| creating zero-tolerance policies, | utilizing empathy-informed choices. |
| | |
| | |

*Note:* What would you add to this list?

## ENABLING CONDITIONS

Often when we talk about student alienation, it is paired with issues outside of our control, such as poverty or a lack of parental involvement. In order to effectively meet the needs of students as risk of dropping out or feeling alienated from the school community, we need to focus on the issues we *can* control. And much to the point I brought up earlier, all students can benefit from social-emotional learning, not just the students who struggle.

In the research around neuroplasticity, Burns (2019) found that "Serotonin is associated with a feeling of well-being and is a powerful modulator of neuroplasticity. As teachers, we are very familiar with the importance of enhancing students' sense of trust and confidence in the educational process, which can help increase serotonin levels in a positive way."

There are a variety of ways that instructional leaders can help students feel safe and supported when they are in school. In my school climate work (2017), I brought in enabling conditions, which I really found when I was doing my doctoral research on safeguarding LGBT students back in 2010. Enabling conditions are simple steps that we can take to ensure that all students feel safe and which, at the same time, help leaders practice instructional leadership. There are two additions to my original list, which I will mention below.

## Enabling Conditions and How You Can Use Them in Your Instructional Leadership Practices

**School board policies/student codes of conduct.** We know that board policies and codes of conduct are important. They provide a roadmap to what a district feels is important, and it gives us the support we need if a parent, student or adult in the community gives us pushback on topics that they consider too controversial to be taught in the school. These topics may include conversations around race, gender or sexual orientation.

Many times leaders will only support what they think is important, and if they don't have the confidence, or self-efficacy, to support safeguards for LGBT students or other marginalized populations, the policy or code of conduct isn't worth the paper it's written on. To make it worth that paper, leaders need to engage in conversations, one-on-one or as a group, with teachers and other leaders who do feel confident speaking about controversial issues. Through that dialogue they can find one starting point. (I'm not asking for leaders to do it all, but I am asking that they do something.)

**Teacher-student relationships.** This is an addition to the enabling conditions, but it is a very important one. In Hattie's synthesis of meta-analysis, teacher-student relationships have an average effect size of .72, which is over the hinge point of .40, which has been shown to equate to a year's worth of growth for a year's input. When students believe we care about them, they will work harder for us, and when they think we don't like them, they will work harder to distance themselves. Students need an emotional connection to their school community, and one of the best ways to provide that is through teacher-student relationships. However, leaders have a stake here too. I provided some examples of how leaders can improve their relationships with students in the five easy steps section of this chapter.

As a principal, I used to greet students getting off the bus, go to every classroom every morning just to say "good morning" to each class, and study the yearbook so that I knew students' names when I saw them in person. Such practices mattered then, and they matter now. As instructional leaders, we can build relationships with students so that they know they can come and talk with us about whatever problem they might face. We may not always know the answers, but we do know how to help them find those answers.

**Mindfulness.** This is a new addition to the list of enabling conditions. The truth is, our students experience a great deal of stress from social media pressures and the goal of getting into a good college. They need to understand how to handle those pressures, because they are beginning to be a normal part of life. Additionally, our teachers and leaders are stressed over the many pressures they feel in their roles. We all need to take time on a daily basis to breathe, have a few moments of silence, and not judge ourselves so negatively.

The research on mindfulness shows that taking time out to breathe can make an enormous difference to how we approach our daily activities.

Mindfulness is not just a recommendation for our students. It is equally as important a recommendation for the adults who work in the school. Given all the trauma and mental health issues that teachers and leaders help students work through, it's easy to see how adults can get caught up in all of this and suffer from vicarious trauma. So, I would like to offer a moment of mindfulness for you in this chapter. Below is a blog post that I wrote for *Finding Common Ground* on mindfulness and adults (DeWitt, 2018b). Please take a moment to breathe and read this piece. This will replace the normal "Mindful Moment" section of the chapter and provide you with a much deeper look at mindfulness. After you finish, we will continue the list of enabling conditions.

## Educators Need Mindfulness. Their Mental Health May Depend on It.

In a very powerful and popular guest post (*Finding Common Ground*, 2018) called "Kids Need Play and Recess. Their Mental Health May Depend on It," superintendent Michael Hynes cites Dr. Peter Gray of Boston College when he writes:

> Peter Gray, a research professor at Boston College, found that "Rates of depression and anxiety among young people in America have been increasing steadily for the past 50 to 70 years. Today, by at least some estimates, five to eight times as many high school and college students meet the criteria for diagnosis of major depression and/or anxiety disorder as was true half a century or more ago." If that doesn't alarm you as a parent, an educator or a concerned citizen, I'm not sure you have a pulse. The fact is, we have an existential mental health crisis in K–12 education and beyond. The question is, what can schools do about it?

It's not just children who are at risk these days.

As a former school principal, and even in my present role as a consultant, I have had a hard time calming down my active mind. I often find myself asking what I should write next, how I can improve on my practice, and what I did wrong to make someone want to provide me with negative feedback.

As a principal and teacher, I often could not shut off the bad interactions I had with colleagues or parents. When I experienced a negative interaction, I would carry it with me like a heavy weight on my shoulders. Do you ever feel that way? If you do, you are clearly not alone.

There are countless school counselors, teachers, nurses and school leaders who feel stress on a daily basis and that begins to bleed into their daily lives. Besides stress, many of these school personnel are working with students who experience trauma at home. Those adults working with this fragile student population are at risk of experiencing vicarious trauma, because they just cannot shake off the heaviness of working with students who seem to be living through so much turmoil.

For example, in "School Counselors' Perceived Stress, Burnout, and Job Satisfaction" (2018, p. 1), Mullen et al. cited numerous studies that showed

*school counselors can face multiple and competing demands, leading to symptoms of stress, empathy fatigue, emotional exhaustion, counselor impairment, and eventual departure or resignation from their jobs.*

When looking at new teachers within their first few years of the profession, McLean et al. (2017, p. 230)

*examined the trajectories of depressive and anxious symptoms among early-career teachers as they transitioned from their training programs into their first year of teaching. In addition, perceived school climate was explored as a moderator of these trajectories. Multilevel linear growth modeling revealed that depressive and anxious symptoms increased across the transition, and negative perceived school climate was related to more drastically increasing symptoms.*

Principals are not immune to stress and burnout either. In fact, Queen and Schumacher (2006) found that

*as many as 75 percent of principals experience stress-related symptoms that include fatigue, weakness, lack of energy, irritability, heartburn, headache, trouble sleeping, sexual dysfunction, and depression.*

Additionally, Van der Merwe and Parsotam (2011) found that *"school principals experience high levels of stress that hamper their self-efficacy and inhibit their executive control capacities."*

### Ten minutes in the morning

What we all have experienced is that when we are busy and feel stressed, even the slightest of things can negatively impact how we move about our day. I used to feel like I woke up in the morning and hit the ground running. The problem is that when we hit the ground running, we sometimes leave ourselves behind.

There are numerous ways to approach the issue of stress and burnout among principals, educators, nurses and counselors. We always should step back and look at how we spend our time. Do we add to our stress by reinventing the wheel each time we have to do a new task; do we look for ways to build collective efficacy because many hands make light work; or do we try to take some of the work off our plate because we spend too much time being martyrs thinking we have to do everything when we really don't?

Besides all of that, do we simply try to give ourselves 10 minutes in the morning and 10 minutes at night to focus on breathing? Yes, 10 minutes.

For full disclosure, I have always been a fan of calming techniques like meditation, but I did not think I was doing it right, so I quit. However, over the last few months I have made a commitment to meditate (I use an app named Calm) for 10 minutes in the morning and 10 at night.

*(Continued)*

(Continued)

You may think that my life as a consultant/author is glamorous. I travel from city to city, meeting wonderful people and seeing amazing places. That's true some of the time, but not all of the time. My life revolves around being in hotels a few times a week about 45 to 47 weeks a year. Participants do not always love being on the receiving end of professional development (surprise!), and I sometimes work all day in one city and get on a plane to travel by night to the next.

Some of the same stress I felt as a consultant mirrored how I felt as a principal and teacher. So, I sat back and learned how to make a conscious effort to breathe in the morning and at night before going to sleep. What I found is that I am less stressed, love the lessons taught by my app, and sleep much, much better. Educators can find the same benefits.

In fact, Van der Merwe and Parsotam found that

*participants' main stressors, their reaction to stress and the influence of controlled breathing on their stress relief were investigated through individual interviewing. It was found that school principals' main stressors related to extensive workloads carried out in an environment of resource constraints. The regular practising of controlled breathing resulted in a decrease of the levels of stress experienced with main improvements related to revitalized energy levels, restored clarity of thinking and improved interpersonal relationships.*

This is supported by the work of Valerie Brown. In a guest post titled "Mindful Leaders Are Key for Transforming Schools" (*Finding Common Ground*, 2016), Brown writes.

*Mindfulness improves a school leader's ability to notice and to focus, slow down, stop, pause, breathe, and avoid automatic reactions that might later cause you regret. The capacity to focus in the moment is a hallmark of leadership excellence. Connecting with others, taking a genuine interest in the well-being of another, listening for what is said and what is left unsaid, supports true understanding and promotes a trustworthy school community. This strengthens the leader's capacity to influence others in a positive way.*

**In the End**

We are all at risk of burnout and stress, which negatively impacts our mental health. Our students need brain breaks and recess in order to ensure that they feel less stress, as Hynes so keenly pointed out, but adults need brain breaks as well, and sometimes it's as easy as waking up in the morning and making breathing a part of our morning routine.

Mindfulness, meditation and breathing may not solve all of our issues, but through the experience of focused breathing, we will become less stressed, sleep better, and take more time to make better decisions which could have positive effects on our mental health. No, this is not rocket science, but sometimes it's the simplest of ideas that have the greatest benefits.

**References**

McLean, L., Abry, T., Taylor, M., Jimenez, M., & Granger, K. (2017, July). Teachers' mental health and perceptions of school climate across the transition from training to teaching. *Teaching and Teacher Education 65*, 230–240.

Mullen, P., Blount, A., Lambie, G., & Chae, N. (2018). School counselors' perceived stress, burnout, and job satisfaction. *Professional School Counseling, 21*(1), 1–10.

Queen, J. A., & Schumacher, D. (2006, November/December). A survival guide for frazzled principals. *Principal*, 18–22.

Van der Merwe, H., & Parsotam, A. (2011, November). School principal stressors and a stress alleviation strategy based on controlled breathing. *Journal of Asian and African Studies, 47*(6), 666–678.

As you can see, social-emotional learning isn't just for students. It's important for adults to take moments to practice mindfulness and foster their own social-emotional health and well-being.

**Inclusive books, novels and curricula.** If we truly want every student to feel that they matter, then we have to have resources to show it. This means using books, novels and curricula that are representative of the diversity within our schools or the diversity we want to prepare our students for in the outside world, and those representations need to be positive. For example, when I was growing up, members of our indigenous population (sometimes referred to as Native Americans) were represented in our textbooks, but it was not a positive representation. These resources can be used to spark healthy debates in classrooms and create important dialogue around inclusivity. This alone is one place leaders can hone their skills as instructional leaders by making sure the curriculum used is inclusive, which helps build student engagement.

**Images.** When you walk into any school, you can see images all over the walls, from student work to colorfully painted murals. Unfortunately, many times those images are representative of only one population within the school, and that population is white, straight students. Images need to represent all students, such as our LGBTQ population, by having Safe Space stickers (Gay, Lesbian, Straight, Education, Network) or murals that include African American, Indian, Latino and Asian students. So many of us are on social media and share pictures because we feel engaged with those images. Shouldn't we offer that same engagement within our schools?

///////////////////////////////////////////////////////////////////////////

## Student Voice Questions

In what ways do you help marginalized students feel valued in your school? What images do they see when they enter the school? Are those images representative of all students?

///////////////////////////////////////////////////////////////////////////

**Professional development for staff.** Self-efficacy is the confidence we feel in ourselves, and research shows that it is context-specific (Tschannen-Moran & Gareis, 2004), meaning that we feel confident about certain parts of our teaching and leadership but completely lack confidence about other parts. Professional development is about building mindfulness around some of those enabling conditions that we find controversial, and it takes more than just one five-minute conversation in one faculty meeting. It means devoting time to making sure our school is truly inclusive. Sometimes that means we have to work with outside professionals, because they hold the expertise. The only thing to keep in mind when working with an outside organization is that its representatives need to understand your school's specific context. All too often, outside organizations enter a school and dictate what needs to happen, which can be a turn-off to staff members. Make sure that those organizations are properly vetted and that they find the right starting point with staff members. When this type of professional development is taking place, it is important that the leader be present and engaged in the learning as well.

**Common language/common understanding.** This is clearly an important topic we discuss throughout the book. It is an enabling condition because we need a common language and common understanding around topics of race, sexual orientation and gender studies.

---

### Mindfulness Moment

In our school where I was a principal in a rural area outside of Albany, New York, we tried to engage students with a calm environment by offering the following changes to how they learned:

**Flexible spaces.** We varied the furniture, offering tables, couches, a tub (yes, a tub), and ball chairs. We wanted to find a balance between a space that distracts and a space that engages.

**Theatre gels.** In many classrooms, we replaced some of the harsh fluorescent overhead lights with theatre gels. They were a soft yellow, orange and blue. Studies show that soft lighting can alleviate anxiety.

**Mindfulness.** We took frequent brain breaks and practiced mindfulness.

**Natural lighting.** There were many windows in our school. Often we turned off the switches and let the sun shine in to light our way.

## In the End

Mental health issues and trauma are critical issues facing leaders in schools around the world. The staggering statistics from the United States, the United Kingdom and Australia show that countless students enter our schools not fully ready to learn. Social-emotional learning may be a controversial topic, and critics believe there isn't a place for it in our schools, but the reality of our time in education is that we cannot neglect to implement social-emotional learning practices. Perhaps this can inspire us to look at why so many children around the world are experiencing trauma and mental health issues, as well as why so many of our students continue to live in poverty. It is our job as educators to try to help them find a way out.

> Social-emotional learning is about empowering all students—those who struggle with mental health issues and those who do not—with the strategies they need to be successful in life.

However, in order to make sure that social-emotional learning does not become the next buzz phrase, like "growth mindset" or "differentiated instruction," we must all agree that SEL is about empowering all students—those who struggle with mental health issues and those who do not—with the strategies they need to be successful in life.

The examples of changing the way we interact with all students might seem like common sense, but the reality is that leaders sometimes get so busy with tasks and pressures that they speak *at* students instead of *with* them. Putting the suggested talking points together with mindfulness, it is my hope that leaders can take a step back and think about their words before they use them with students. This is especially important when considering the research around alienation. It's not just grading practices or our curriculum that might alienate students. Sometimes it could merely be the way we interact with them in our conversations.

It is my hope that changing the way we talk with students, and finding ways to make sure we engage our marginalized populations, will help combat all of this trauma students feel. In order to help you do these things, I have used the program logic model from earlier in the book and adapted it for social-emotional learning. As with all program logic models you will find represented in this book, Figure 4.4 provides specific details that will help meet the needs of the school, which in this case are ways to build an emotional connection to the school community. I truly hope it helps you move forward in a positive way.

Figure 4.4    Program Logic Model Example: Building Social-Emotional Engagement

## Social-Emotional Engagement

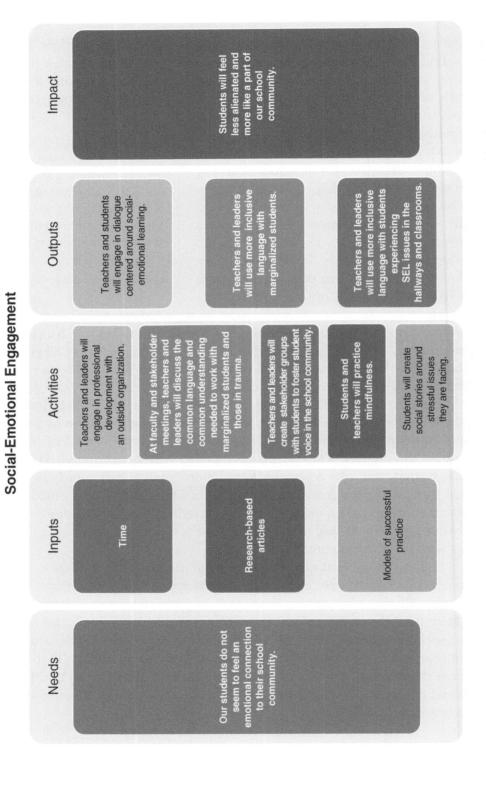

## STUDY GUIDE QUESTIONS

- As a leadership group, how do you foster a more inclusive climate where students feel engaged socially and emotionally? What are specific examples you can offer?
- How have poverty and trauma impacted your school system? What supports do you have in place as far as these are concerned? Are they working?
- How do you achieve a balance between (a) understanding the needs of students experiencing traumatic issues and (b) challenging them with the academic education they need?
- Think together about ways in which practices in your school (lack of inclusive resources, grading practices, etc.) may be alienating some students. How might your group help foster a climate where students feel less alienated?
- When it comes to enabling conditions, how does your school, district or school board (Canada) make sure that the resources used in teaching are inclusive for all students? If your first reaction is to skip this question, perhaps you should look deeper into that.
- Out of the enabling conditions offered in this chapter, which ones do you believe your leadership team excels at, and which ones might be an area of growth for all of you?

# INSTRUCTIONAL STRATEGIES

## Exploring Surface, Deep, and Transfer Learning

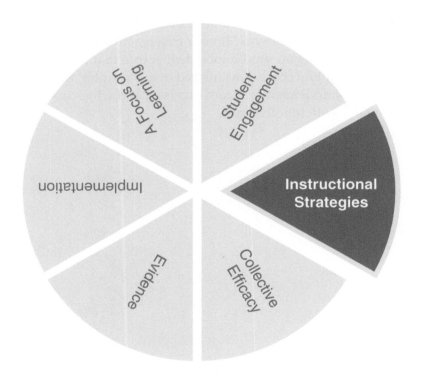

Scan this QR code for a video introduction to the chapter.

When I taught first grade in a high-poverty city school, I was in the process of being formally observed by our assistant principal. I typically appreciated his observations, and I believed he had the credibility to provide me with feedback and insight based on his experience as an elementary teacher himself. One time when he entered my classroom at the scheduled time, I decided to change the plan from what we had agreed on during our pre-conference meeting to something I thought would be much more beneficial to him to see. I also thought it would be good for the students, because it would help them see why we do what we do every day. To be honest, it was not a premeditated decision; it was an idea that came to me quickly.

The problem with observations is that they provide a snapshot of a moment in time. If a principal doesn't enter classrooms frequently, then that snapshot may be accurate or inaccurate, depending on how the lesson goes. As much as I liked the assistant principal, I felt as though he was not able to see the day-to-day teaching and learning that went on in my classroom. In fact, he only entered my classroom when he needed something or for the two observations he was required to complete. That isn't a judgment; it's a reality.

As he sat down to start writing notes, I told the students we were going to do our usual center-based cooperative learning a bit differently. I asked them to help me highlight our daily ELA practices for the assistant principal in the 45 minutes he would spend with us on that day. I asked questions about our Monday learning, which a few students began to answer. I then moved on to Tuesday, and then Wednesday. As I dove into the content for each day, more and more students began to engage, and I found that our assistant principal began to ask more and more questions the students could answer. It didn't feel like a risk where the assistant principal was concerned, because I never felt like he was going to give me fewer points because I changed direction. However, it was a risk where the students were concerned, because in that moment I was about to find out whether they really understood what we did every day. If they couldn't answer the questions, were my center-based learning practices as great as I thought they were? Fortunately, I found out in that moment that we were a well-oiled machine.

## Mindful Moment

Reflect on the observations that you do with teachers. Do you encourage them to break away from the lesson and be more spontaneous? If not, why?

> The goal of an instructional leader is to lower our perceived status as a principal and raise the status of those around us. It involves creating spaces of dialogue around learning to respect the expertise of the teachers.

The goal of an instructional leader is to lower our perceived status as a principal and raise the status of those around us. It involves creating spaces of dialogue around learning to respect the expertise of the teachers. In my work as a principal, I wanted to offer those same incredible moments of creativity that I was allowed to have with my assistant principal back when I was a teacher. How do we create moments to show how we are a well-oiled machine in our schools? All of this involves a deep understanding of academic engagement and instructional strategies.

## ACADEMIC ENGAGEMENT

Academic engagement is a multidimensional theoretical construct that comprises three components: behavioral, emotional, and cognitive engagement (Wilcox, McQuay, Blackstaffe, Perry, & Hawe, 2018, p. 180). We have already explored behavioral and emotional engagement, so this chapter will focus on cognitive engagement, which is an area of critical need for instructional leaders. As a first-grade teacher, I was fortunate to work with 6- and 7-year-old students, because I had to find a balance between cognitive engagement and keeping young children actively engaged. It was not always an easy job. Nor is it easy to always engage middle-school students, and high-school students, and it requires the combined effort of teachers and principals.

In a study completed by the National Association of Elementary School Principals (Fuller et al., 2018, p. 33), over 82% of principals said that they had seen an increase in the amount of time they were spending on assessment data and instructional strategies with teachers. Although this may be a relatively new role for building leaders, academic engagement needs to be a part of the conversations.

The use of instructional strategies to increase academic engagement is well-researched and is based on some important assumptions. In fact, Coates (2005) focused on the importance of using a range of activities in the classroom and how those activities impact student engagement.

> The concept of student engagement is based on the . . . assumption that learning is influenced by how an individual participates in educationally purposeful activities. . . . In essence, therefore, student engagement is concerned with the extent to which students are engaging in a range of educational activities that research has shown as likely to lead to high quality learning. (p. 26)

Student engagement is easy to talk about but much harder to do. The reality is that some of our students do not come to school actively engaged. It takes work, but we need to remember that they are coming to school every day for a reason, and we need to work hard to find ways to engage them. I honestly always found that my least engaged students were my biggest challenge, but they were the ones who taught me the most about my own teaching.

In a national survey of more than 600 school teachers conducted by the Education Week Research Center (2014), only 4 in 10 said that the majority of students in their schools were highly engaged and motivated (p. 3). Motivating students should be one of the most exciting parts of an educator's job. Perhaps a reason for the reported lack of student enthusiasm was that, as more than half of the respondents in the same study indicated, their preservice teaching programs had not prepared them to engage and motivate students (p. 3).

> **Mindful Moment**
>
> When I was a K–12 student myself, I was a struggling learner (i.e., retained in elementary school, graduated ranked 262 out of 266 from high school). When you think about engagement, what engaged *you* as a K–12 student? Do you use that experience to help guide you as an instructional leader?

In order to combine the topic of academic engagement with instructional strategies, let's reflect on an earlier conversation around knowledge dimensions. As we learned in Chapter 3, there are four knowledge dimensions that we have to understand in order to combine the topics of academic engagement and instructional strategies. See Figure 5.1 for a review.

In the following pages, I'm going to break down several high-impact teaching strategies. We'll discuss what they should look like, talk about whether they can be used for surface-, deep- or transfer-level learning, and

**Figure 5.1**   The Four Knowledge Dimensions

| Knowledge Dimension | |
|---|---|
| Factual | Factual knowledge includes isolated bits of information, such as vocabulary definitions and knowledge about specific details. |
| Conceptual | Conceptual knowledge consists of systems of information, such as classifications and categories. |
| Procedural | Procedural knowledge involves knowledge of skills, such as how to carry out a task. |
| Metacognitive | Metacognitive knowledge refers to knowledge of thinking processes and information about how to manipulate these processes effectively. |

Based on research by Anderson and Krathwohl (2001b) and Stern et al. (2018).

match them up with the appropriate knowledge dimension. The reason for this is to help instructional leaders understand how these strategies are supposed to be implemented, but also to help create some clarity about what to look for in walkthroughs and informal and formal teacher observations.

To illustrate just how important clarity around instructional strategies is, I'd like to share with you my blog post titled "The Myth of Walkthroughs," from the *Finding Common Ground* blog (DeWitt, 2016b). Please pay close attention to several of the strategies that you normally look for in classrooms and learn why the need for clarity around them is necessary.

---

### The Myth of Walkthroughs: Eight Unobserved Practices in Classrooms

Walkthroughs are pretty popular these days. A principal, or a team of administrators and teacher leaders, walk through a group of classrooms and look for certain instructional practices. After they're completed, the team provides feedback to the teacher. In schools where walkthroughs are done correctly, teachers and leaders work together, have agreed upon or co-constructed the "*look for*" that should be taking place in the classrooms, and have dialogue around the feedback.

   *In other cases...walkthroughs aren't so popular or positive.*

This may happen because the school leader and teachers do not work collaboratively. The principal never co-constructed what to look for with teachers, and the teachers are not told beforehand. The walkthroughs are more about compliance, and therefore the success of walkthroughs is more of a myth than a reality.

There are leaders who say they are doing walkthroughs, when in actuality, they have never shared the focus, or the form, they're using with the teacher . . . and the teacher doesn't receive any effective feedback.

When completing a Visible Learning (Hattie) capability assessment in Melbourne, Australia, in February, there was a school leader who co-constructed the walkthrough goals with teachers, and every week he hung up a regular-sized gold sign in the faculty room, the main office, and the main hallway near his office. The sign provided the walkthrough focus of the week so everyone was aware of what it was, and there had been a team involved who established each focus area.

#### Relational Trust

Unfortunately, walkthroughs have not been done in the spirit for which they were inspired, so teachers don't feel that they can trust the process. Leaders often feel as though the practice is more successful than teachers do. That's where the important work of Bryk and Schneider that centers around relational trust comes into the equation.

In *Trust in Schools: A Core Resource for School Reform* (Educational Leadership. ASCD), Bryk and Schneider write,

*Distinct role relationships characterize the social exchanges of schooling: teachers with students, teachers with other teachers, teachers with parents, and all groups with the school principal. Each party in a relationship maintains an understanding of his or her role's obligations and holds some expectations about the obligations of the other parties. For a school community to work well, it must achieve agreement in each role relationship in terms of the understandings held about these personal obligations and expectations of others.*

In order for all of us to move on and work effectively, especially if leaders continue to use walkthroughs as a way to gauge what is happening in classrooms around the school, we must all have a common understanding of what works and what may need to be tweaked in our classrooms. We need the myth often related to the success of walkthroughs to become more of a reality.

There are at least eight areas that leaders don't often look for in their walkthroughs, or if they do, it's at a very surface level. It's one of the reasons why John Hattie, someone I work with as a Visible Learning trainer, has shown in his research that some of our favorite strategies to use in the classroom don't have the positive effect we think they do. We often don't approach these strategies as deeply as we could.

**The eight practices are:**

**Cooperative learning vs. cooperative seating.** Leaders and teachers talk about it. We know it's important for students to work cooperatively. However, professor and researcher Rob Coe (2004) found that we put students in cooperative groups over 70% of the time they are in our classrooms, but they are spending 80% of that time working on individual activities. We have to be careful that when we provide the myth that students are engaging in cooperative learning, it doesn't actually mean they are just participating in cooperative seating.

**Authentic engagement vs. compliant engagement.** Just because students are following the speaker or answering a question doesn't mean they are actively and authentically engaged. Read the comments on [my blog post "Student Engagement: Is It Authentic or Compliant" at https://blogs.edweek.org/edweek/finding_common_ground/2016/04/student_engagement_is_it_authentic_or_compliant.html] because there are some great resources that readers offered.

**Surface-level vs. deep-level questioning.** A teacher may establish a goal with a coach to look at whether their questions are more surface level than deep. Do we scaffold our questions, or do we spend most of our time asking questions most of the students already know the answers to?

*(Continued)*

(Continued)

**Teacher talk vs. student talk.** University of Melbourne researcher Janet Clinton found that on average, teachers asked about 200 questions per day and students asked two questions per student per week. The part that may be even more disturbing? Our high-achieving students are okay with this, because they can weed through what is important and what is not. Our struggling students, on the other hand, want the teacher to stop so they can talk it out with a peer who can explain it to them in a more student-friendly language.

**Teacher-student relationships.** Hattie's research found that positive teacher-student relationships can have an effect size of .72, which is almost double the hinge point of .40 (which indicates a year's worth of growth for a year's input). In walkthroughs, do we make time to talk about the enormous impact that our relationships have on our students?

**Growth vs. fixed mindset.** I'm a fan of Dweck's work, but even she believes that too many schools say they're a growth mindset school when they aren't. Hattie's research shows that the growth vs. fixed mindset has an effect size of .19. The myth is that school leaders say they are a growth mindset school when they're still treating students in fixed ways.

**One-to-one initiatives.** There is a commercial in Albany, NY, where I live. It's of a K–8 school, and one of the highlights of paying to have your children attend this school is that they will get their own tablet, because the school has a one-to-one initiative. I'm not against one-to-one initiatives, but I have visited far too many schools where students are using tablets to complete a worksheet. Instead of using a pencil, they can type on their tablet. That's not really all the more engaging than using a pencil. It's supposed to be about curation and not just consumption.

**Walkthroughs.** Walkthroughs are not always as deep as we want people to think they are. In schools, teachers do not always know what the walkthroughs are focusing on, and the leaders don't always offer effective feedback after they are completed. Too many times, the success of walkthroughs is a myth, because they focus on compliant behavior and making sure teachers are covering curriculum. Walkthroughs will be much more successful if they bring about deep learning on the part of students, teachers and the leaders who are doing them.

### In the End

We should not be overly concerned with the methods we use in the classroom, at least not as much as we should be concerned with how much of an impact they are having on student learning. Buzzwords and buzz phrases crop up in every profession, but we are spending too much time creating myths that may not be true. Let's start spending more time scratching the surface to see if we really do what we say we do.

Walkthroughs may be a good way to help bring that to light, but they will only be beneficial if the relationships we have in place with our teacher colleagues, the school climate, the way we listen to students, and the feedback we give and get from each other are authentic and not compliant.

**References**

Bryk, A. S., & Schneider, B. (2003, March). Trust in schools: A core resource for school reform. *Educational Leadership, 60*(6, "Creating Caring Schools"), 40–45. https://www.ascd.org/publications/educational-leadership/mar03/vol60/num06/Trust-in-Schools@-A-Core-Resource-for-School-Reform.aspx

Coe, R. (2004). *(Classroom) observation* [slideshow presentation]. Retrieved from https://www.slideshare.net/haryshahn/6-classroom-observation-17670761

Hattie, J. (2018). *Visible Learning. 250+ influences on learning: Cognition education.* Thousand Oaks, CA: Corwin Press.

I would like to be clear that the work I do is not about getting leaders and teachers to stop doing anything. What I want is for leaders and teachers to reflect on what they are doing with the evidence available to them and go deeper with it if it is working.

The following three strategies are meant to provide teachers and leaders with clarity and help give students a voice in the classroom. My intention is to provide an understanding around each strategy, describe which level of learning (i.e., surface, deep, or transfer) it will help students achieve, and relate it to the knowledge dimension content we focused on in Chapter 3.

Teacher clarity is the place to begin, because learning and student engagement all begins with how clear we are as teachers in the classroom.

## TEACHER CLARITY

Fendick (1990, p. 2) found that teacher clarity takes place when the teacher explains the subject matter of the lesson "in such a way that it is easy for the students to understand." Ways in which teachers can achieve this are to "explain things simply and make them interesting" and to "repeat and stress directions and difficult points, introduce new content in small steps and relate it to content that has been already mastered by the students" (p. 2). Fendick further advises that lessons be conducted "at a pace appropriate to the topic and to the students" (p. 3).

Bush, Kennedy, and Cruickshank (1977, pp. 55–56) found that there are five factors that contribute to a greater sense of clarity. Those five factors, which represent clear targets, are as follows:

**Factor 1**—*Explaining through written and verbal examples*

- Giving written and oral examples, staying on topic, using common examples, and so on

**Factor 2**—*Personalizing using multiple strategies*

- Explaining by telling a story
- Having students make outlines
- Repeating information, for students who need it repeated

**Factor 3**—*Task orientation*, which will provide and assure student understanding

- Talking only about those things that are related to the topic of the lesson
- Giving the students consistent (i.e., daily) practice
- Finishing the lesson without stopping in the middle

**Factor 4**—*Verbal fluency*

- Using grammatically correct speech
- Providing specific details

**Factor 5**—*Organizing student work*

- Encouraging students to take notes

**Levels of learning.** Teacher clarity can be used for surface-, deep-, and transfer-level learning.

**Knowledge dimensions.** Teacher clarity can be used for factual, conceptual, procedural, and metacognitive dimensions of learning.

Teacher clarity, further, includes the use of learning intentions, which involve stating the goal of the lesson, and success criteria, which means providing students with a clear idea of what successful learning will look like. Hattie has often suggested that teacher clarity is enhanced when teachers and students develop success criteria together. However, it is equally as important to note that teachers should not post countless learning intentions and success criteria on their classroom walls—it can be confusing or

### Mindful Moment

Here is an activity I learned from my former school superintendent Jo Moccia. Give every teacher in a faculty meeting a plain piece of college-ruled paper. Have them close their eyes, explain that they do not have time for questions (even say you are short on time), and then give them the following directions:

- Fold the paper in half.
- Rip the top right-hand corner.
- Fold the paper in half again.
- Rip the middle.
- Open your eyes.

Every time I have done this activity with an audience, the papers come out looking different. Why? Because some people will fold length-wise; others, by width. Some rip a larger section of the top right-hand corner. The point of all this is to illustrate that, as teachers, we know the directions, but students may not all understand them in the same way. If we are not clear, due to things like lack of time or trying to do too much, the students will not gain the same sense of learning.

overwhelming, or students may begin to take less notice simply because this "wall art" is everywhere. I have entered many classes that have learning intentions and success criteria plastered around the walls. When I asked students in those classrooms what the learning intentions and success criteria were, many could not provide the answer.

Teacher clarity is what is needed in order to provide a deep understanding in our classrooms. It helps set the foundation for all lessons, and as you can see from the research behind it, this concept of teacher clarity has been around for many decades.

After teachers and leaders focus on teacher clarity, they can then dive into other teaching strategies that will help engage students academically and socially-emotionally. The next teaching strategy is that of classroom discussion. As you may have noticed in "The Myth of Walkthroughs," I used the research of Janet Clinton out of the University of Melbourne, which showed that teachers often ask their students 200 questions per day while fielding only two questions per student per week. Classroom discussion is a strategy for bringing more balance to that dialogue.

## CLASSROOM DISCUSSION

Witherspoon, Sykes, and Bell (2016) define classroom discussion as "a sustained exchange between and among teachers and their students with the purpose of developing students' capabilities or skills and/or expanding students' understanding—both shared and individual—of a specific concept or instructional goal" (p. 6).

Classroom discussion can help students build a conceptual understanding, and it provides such a great opportunity for teachers and leaders to engage in formative assessment about the level of understanding in the classroom.

Witherspoon et al. (2016) go on to clarify that the essential elements of effective classroom discussions are:

- high quality and high quantities of student talk;
- questioning of students; taking up, revoicing, and pressing students' ideas; structuring and steering the conversation toward the learning goal(s); and
- enabling students to respond to one another's ideas by stepping back to listen, moderate and facilitate students' interactions, ensuring that the content under discussion is represented accurately, and bringing the discussion to a meaningful close.

There are numerous ways to engage in classroom discussion. Gonzalez (2015) highlights the following strategies for stimulating classroom discussion, and I will explain each one:

**Gallery walks.** One method involves having students work in partners or groups on a learning task that they then hang up on the wall, sometimes using chart paper. The students all stand up and walk around the classroom, with the learning intention and success criteria in mind, and add feedback to each of the pieces of chart paper. Using the Padlet app or Google Slides can help teachers and students incorporate technology into this activity and help deepen the learning on the part of all the students, because students can include links in their discussion and feedback.

**Socratic seminar.** The teacher assigns a specific reading passage or group of passages to students before class, and then they come to the next class prepared for a discussion. This can sometimes be referred to as the Flipped Model, because students are given pre-work that helps them build knowledge around an idea. Perhaps the teacher uses conceptual understanding methods by asking what the relationship is between what they read and a real-life example. Utilizing technology in a Socratic seminar may mean that you have two classes from different schools get together using video-conferencing software such as Skype, Zoom or Google Hangout. Other times Socratic seminar can be done in virtual classes. In the course I teach at the University of Oklahoma, we have used Facebook to pose a question online and have students post their answers during class, on a break, or after the class has finished meeting in person.

**Affinity mapping.** Gonzalez (2015) writes that, for this strategy, the teacher should "[g]ive students a broad question or problem that is likely to result in lots of different ideas, such as 'What were the impacts of the Great Depresssion?' or 'What literary works should every person read?'" Students are usually tasked with writing a single response on a sticky note, and then they stick all the responses on the wall. They then consider the responses and move them around to organize them by theme. It's easy to incorporate technology into this activity by using online mapping boards, which are offered by a whole host of organizations.

**Backchannel discussions.** Backchanneling happens during or after a lecture or discussion. Perhaps the teacher or a student shared information through a presentation or YouTube video where they focused on the reason for the American Civil War. After students are given time to reflect on what they learned, the teacher or a student can create a question on a backchannel like "What is the relationship between issues that contributed to the Civil War and issues our country is facing today?" Students engage in a discussion outside of the normal lecture using a tool like Google Classroom, Padlet or Backchannel Chat (I sometimes shudder when adding names of tech tools, because they go out of fashion so quickly and new ones pop up all the time. For the most current way to offer a backchannel discussion, teachers can search for one using their favorite search engine). Backchanneling encourages reflection and offers an opportunity for those students who are too shy to speak up or don't like to be called on the opportunity to reflect on their learning and offer feedback.

**Levels of learning.** As you may have guessed, all of these classroom discussion techniques can be used for surface-, deep- and transfer-level learning. Additionally, they fit into the conceptual understanding work that was explained in Chapter 3.

**Knowledge dimensions.** Classroom discussion can be used for factual, conceptual, procedural and metacognitive dimensions of learning.

Classroom discussion is highly engaging and provides an opportunity for teachers to sit back and relax a bit more and let their students speak up. Cold-calling students, which is when teachers stand and deliver content and then call on students without warning, does not always work well, because students may not feel confident enough to quickly answer questions flying at them from a teacher. These classroom discussion strategies offered above are some valuable ways to get students to participate and engage in dialogue with each other.

## Student Voice Questions

How often are students involved in authentic discussions when you enter classrooms for formal observations or walkthroughs? Do you sit down next to students and listen in to their discussions around learning?

Another way to go from surface to deep levels of learning that will ultimately offer transfer-level benefits is that of metacognition, which will be the last teaching strategy offered in this chapter.

## METACOGNITION

Flavell (1979, p. 906) writes, "Metacognitive knowledge is one's stored knowledge or beliefs about oneself and others as cognitive agents, about tasks, about actions or strategies, and about how all these interact to affect the outcomes of any sort of intellectual enterprise." Over the years, research has suggested that this has an enormous impact on student learning. Flavell (1979, p. 906) goes on to say, "Metacognitive experiences are conscious cognitive or affective experiences that occur during the enterprise and concern any aspect of it—often, how well it is going." Much more simply, metacognition is the way we think about our own thinking.

There are two processes going on in our heads when it comes to learning how to learn.

1. **Knowledge of cognition** involves awareness of factors that influence our own individual learning, having a collection of strategies to use that supports our own learning, and choosing the appropriate strategy.
2. **Regulation of cognition** includes the ever popular setting goals and planning, as well as monitoring our learning, and evaluating whether our chosen strategy is working—and, if it is not working, then making some sort of adjustment (Centre for Innovation and Excellence in Learning, n.d.)

Following are some very useful metacognitive strategies to use with students.

**Think-alouds.** Students are taught how to talk out loud during their learning activity. They verbalize the steps they are taking and why they are taking those steps. This can be done with thought partners, who are peer partners in learning. Thought partners are peers who can ask questions of each other to deepen the level of learning.

**Concept mapping.** This is also sometimes referred to as "mind mapping," and it involves students taking key words or key concepts and placing them around a paper or an online tool. Subtopics are often brought in and there is a line or connection drawn from the main concept to the subtopic. A very innovative way to create concept maps these days is through sketchnotes, which are highly popular on social media or at education conferences.

**Self-questioning.** This is clearly very similar to think-alouds, because it involves students questioning themselves when they are solving a problem and are hit with a challenge. This process helps them deepen their understanding of the concept that they are learning about.

**Self-monitoring.** This involves the ability to track our thoughts when we are learning. Very often teachers may use checklists with students that the students will then begin to use on their own. Checklists allow students a way to monitor their thinking when they are alone in their learning.

Metacognitive activities are at the deepest level of learning. They take a great deal of modeling on the part of the teacher, and they take a lot of time for trial and error for students. In order for students to enter into some of these metacognitive activities, they need to have a deep understanding of the concept at hand.

Within each of those three highlighted examples of instructional strategies are a few deeper strategies. All of this is meant to help instructional leaders understand what to look for when they are doing walkthroughs or completing formal and informal teacher observations. However,

> **Levels of learning.** Metacognition is specifically used for deep- and transfer-level learning. Additionally, these strategies fit into the conceptual understanding work that was explained in Chapter 3.
>
> **Knowledge dimensions.** Besides metacognitive dimensions of learning, they can also be used for conceptual and procedural dimensions of learning.

they are equally as important to use as discussion points in faculty, staff, PLC and department meetings with teachers. If instructional leaders are going to look for these strategies in the classroom, they should never do it without first having a dialogue about them with teachers and students.

////////////////////////////////////////////////////////////////////////////.

## Student Voice Questions

Do you believe that students of all ages understand metacognition? Do teachers in your school actively discuss metacognitive strategies with students?

////////////////////////////////////////////////////////////////////////////

All of these strategies, and their connection to knowledge dimensions and levels of learning, are meant to highlight the issue of student academic engagement. Claxton (2007, pp. 123–128) offers instructional leaders strategies based on his research focusing on deepening learner engagement. Those strategies involve:

**Language.** Use clear academic language to help elevate student vocabulary. Claxton refers to this as our ability to speak "learnish."

**Activities.** Claxton suggests that learning should be both attractive and challenging.

**Split-screen thinking.** Just as we referred to in other sections of this book, we need to keep both content and process in mind.

**Wild topics.** Students learn best when the topics are both rich and real. Discussion of the subject being taught needs to connect to their world.

**Transparency and involvement.** Claxton writes, "The goal of expanding students' learning capacity seems more likely to take root in a school culture if students understand what is going on, and are given some significant role in helping to design and bring about the desired culture change" (p. 126).

**Transfer thinking.** Learning needs to connect with a greater good.

**Progression.** The learning needs to go to a much broader and deeper level of learning. It involves and revolves around expectations. There is an expectation that learning needs to become more complex as students mature across grade levels and content areas.

**Modeling.** We learn from those whom we surround ourselves with. As leaders and teachers, we need to share our challenges, and how we overcome them, with students. We also need to approach life not just from the knowing mindset, but from a learning mindset as well (Claxton, 2007, pp. 123–128).

Lastly, I have included our program logic model to illustrate how an instructional leader might implement a new model of academic engagement and instructional strategies that will help the school meet that goal. See Figure 5.2.

As you can see, the sample program logic model involves reading research-based articles. It also involves providing examples of strategies, which might include utilizing YouTube or Teaching Channel videos to help show what those strategies look like in practice. For this program logic model, there is a specific focus on Claxton's research around engagement.

From the necessary inputs, you can see the activities that will help best educate the group on engagement practices. This is particularly important, considering the aforementioned *Education Week* study in which less than half of teachers stated that their preservice teaching programs had prepared them for academic engagement. Lastly, you can see that the outputs, outcomes and impact focus on increased academic engagement and an increase in dialogue between teachers and their students.

The program logic model is easy to put together but takes time to roll out. It takes even more time to implement strategies and see student engagement increase. However, the collaboration it takes to build the program logic model will help deepen the level of that implementation and could ultimately lead to collective efficacy and a fantastic impact on academic engagement.

## IN THE END

Claxton has a great quotation that I will leave you with in this chapter: "If Vygotsky is right that, to put it crudely, you pick up your mental habits from the people around you, then we want young people to be around adults, and other

Figure 5.2   Program Logic Model Example: Building Academic Engagement

**Academic Engagement**

| Needs | Inputs | Activities | Outputs | Impact |
|---|---|---|---|---|
| Research-based articles on academic engagement | Research-based articles | PLC meetings will be used to create a common understanding around "academic engagement." | Groups of teachers will pilot teacher clarity strategies. | We will see an increase in academic engagement among our students. |
| Examples of different instructional strategies | Models of successful practices | PLC will engage in a deep discussion of Claxton's engagement strategies and reflect on which strategies they are already using. | Part of teacher clarity will be to utilize strategies that increase classroom discussion. | |
| Read Claxton's article on engagement | Time to discuss the concept of academic engagement | Instructional leader will attend PLC discussions and talk with teachers about which elements should be included on walkthrough feedback form. | Principal's walkthroughs will help provide feedback incorporating Claxton's strategies to increase student engagement. | |
| Create surveys asking students how they believe they best learn | | Send surveys to the students in the classrooms where the pilot program will take place. | | |

students, who are themselves paragons of learning, rather than of knowing" (2007, pp. 123–128). In this chapter, we focused on ways of demonstrating how to learn, rather than simply attempting to transmit knowledge. Being an instructional leader is about understanding academic engagement and then focusing on the instructional strategies that will help build that engagement. Three of the areas that we highlighted are teacher clarity, classroom discussion and metacognition. Within those three areas we discussed a variety of strategies that will help attain each goal of student academic engagement.

Additionally, I felt it was important to highlight the myths surrounding walkthroughs. I know we have talked about this popular instructional leadership strategy before, but it bears repeating that walkthroughs must be approached correctly. Instructional leaders should never engage in walkthroughs without engaging in dialogue with teachers about them. Instructional leadership is not about being a compliance officer—it's about being a partner in learning. With that partnership in mind, Chapter 6 explores yet another component of instructional leadership, and that is efficacy.

## STUDY GUIDE QUESTIONS

- At the beginning of the chapter, I provided an example of how I changed my teaching plan as soon as the assistant principal entered my classroom for a formal observation. How often does your leadership team encourage teachers to break away from a lesson and be spontaneous, especially during a formal observation?
- The NAESP study showed us that principals are seeing an increase in the amount of time they spend talking about assessment and learning. How does your leadership team focus on the same type of data?
- *Education Week*'s study showed that 6 in 10 teachers believe their students are not highly motivated. How might you use that information to help guide a discussion around student engagement?
- How do you engage with teachers in dialogue around walkthroughs?
- Of the three instructional strategies highlighted in this section (i.e., teacher clarity, classroom discussion, and metacognition), which one do you see used the most in your school?
- What is the relationship between Claxton's research strategies and what is happening in your school?
- How might your team go about creating a program logic model to implement new instructional strategies to increase academic engagement?

# 6

# COLLECTIVE EFFICACY

## Easy to Define, Hard to Build?

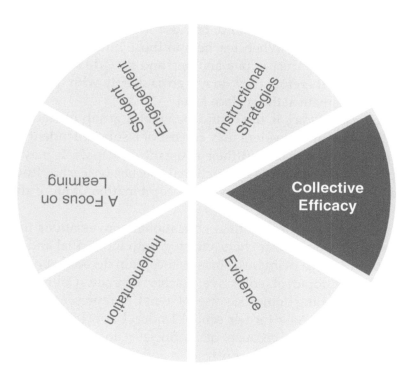

Instructional Strategies

Collective Efficacy

Evidence

Implementation

A Focus on Learning

Student Engagement

Scan this QR code for a video introduction to the chapter.

There are four areas of efficacy that are important to the topic of instructional leadership. Although I will provide a short summary of each at the beginning of this chapter, I will go deeper into each one as this chapter unfolds.

*Self-efficacy* is the confidence we have in ourselves. If we lack confidence in a particular area of pursuit, we are more than likely going to avoid that area because we are worried that we will not be able to do it right. After all, we're human, and many of us want to be seen as competent adults. It's unfortunate that we don't have more of a growth mindset, where we want to dive into challenges that take us out of our comfort zones. A good leader can help us get over that fear and try something new.

*Leadership efficacy* is the confidence that leaders have in themselves. It's important to separate that out from other types of efficacy, because leadership is important. We often wonder why some leaders seem to take on challenges with a great deal of energy, while others seem to avoid challenges and remain in their office. I will explain that a little deeper in this chapter.

*Collective teacher efficacy* is the confidence that a group of teachers have in one another. It is not easy to build, because some school climates are fractured and they lack trust. When teachers in those buildings come together, they often do not have trust in one another, and they do not challenge each other's thinking, so therefore they do not go as deeply with their learning as they could. They remain at the surface level.

*Collective leader efficacy* is the confidence that a group of leaders have in each other. That group of leaders may consist of a superintendent and his or her principals, or principals and their assistant principals. It may also be a leadership group that involves instructional coaches or teacher leaders. Collective leader efficacy may even involve a combination of all of the groups that I just mentioned.

Efficacy is the topic of countless educational conversations these days. For some educators and researchers, efficacy, both individual and collective, has always been an area of interest since its inception decades ago.

Let's take the topic of collective teacher efficacy. Collective teacher efficacy is a fascinating topic because of what it represents for teachers, leaders and students. As a former school leader, I appreciate the power of collective teacher efficacy because, at its finest, it fosters an experience in which teachers work together, construct a common goal around learning, and do the necessary work to achieve that goal. When hearing this, you might almost envision the members of an Olympic rowing team working together to propel themselves almost effortlessly across the water. However, what is even more interesting to me than the power of collective teacher efficacy is the fact that collective teacher efficacy has become one of the biggest challenges for leaders.

While doing the research for my leadership coaching book *Coach It Further*, I surveyed more than 300 school leaders and found that there were four challenges that leaders were most concerned about: communication, community engagement, the political issues that arise in schools, and collective teacher efficacy (DeWitt, 2018a). Survey respondents stated that they found it hard to practice instructional leadership because of these four areas of challenge.

As I began doing research for that book around instructional leadership, I surveyed more than 350 school principals, and collective teacher efficacy came up as the top area of focus for the leaders (DeWitt, 2019) focusing on instructional leadership. In fact, out of 350 respondents, 150 ranked collective teacher efficacy as their number one area of interest when it comes to instructional leadership. It's interesting to think that one topic can be on a list of the necessary components of instructional leadership and yet show up on the list of challenges that leaders worry about the most. However, when you think about it, it really makes sense. Sometimes those things that compose our biggest areas of interest can become some of our biggest challenges. To be honest, though, some leaders limit their ability to build collective efficacy because they do not look at all the ways in which it can be built, and often they believe it is about teachers working with teachers. Let's explore that notion and discover other ways that collective efficacy can be built.

## COLLECTIVE TEACHER EFFICACY: A DEFINITION

Tschannen-Moran and Barr (2004) define collective teacher efficacy as the "collective self-perception that teachers in a given school make an educational difference to their students over and above the educational impact of their homes and communities." Self-efficacy is the confidence we have in ourselves, and collective teacher efficacy is the confidence we have in our group. However, that collective confidence needs to have a positive impact on student learning. If the group together doesn't have a positive impact on student learning, then it isn't collective teacher efficacy. Additionally, it's that *"collective self-perception"* that Tschannen-Moran and Barr included in their definition that can prove difficult, because the diverse members of a group sometimes have to work hard to arrive at that collective self-perception.

Goddard, Hoy, and Hoy (2004) found, "The connections between collective efficacy beliefs and student outcomes depend in part on the reciprocal relationships among these collective efficacy beliefs, teachers' personal sense of efficacy, teachers' professional practice, and teachers' influence over instructionally relevant school decisions" (p. 3). All of this is what makes collective efficacy so difficult to build, but the work is worth it in the long run, because the journey is sometimes equally as important as the final destination.

////////////////////////////////////////////////////////////////////////

## Student Voice Questions

Did you know that students can develop collective efficacy as well? When students work together and it impacts their learning in a positive way, it is collective efficacy. How do students work together in classrooms around the school you lead? And, in order for it to be considered collective efficacy, what evidence do teachers collect to see whether that collective work had a positive impact on student learning?

////////////////////////////////////////////////////////////////////////

Well-known psychologist Albert Bandura is often seen as the godfather of efficacy. Bandura (1977, 1986) found four experiences that shape self-efficacy and collective efficacy. These are *mastery experiences, vicarious experiences, social persuasion,* and *affective states.*

**Mastery experiences.** Mastery experiences offer the biggest impact to efficacy. A mastery experience is the most powerful source of efficacy information (Goddard et al., 2004). Goddard et al. (2004) found that "the perception that a performance has been successful tends to raise efficacy beliefs, contributing to the expectation that performance will be proficient in the future. The perception that one's performance has been a failure tends to lower efficacy beliefs, contributing to the expectation that future performances will also be inept" (p. 5). If someone believes that their performance was successful, they will continue to put forth that same type of effort in the future. If they didn't feel it was successful, they will probably begin to shy away from giving the same amount of effort.

**Vicarious experiences.** This simply means we learn when things are modeled for us. However, where this gets a bit tricky is that the person doing the modeling must have credibility in our eyes. If the person sharing a best practice doesn't have credibility to us, then we are most likely not going to learn from them.

**Social persuasion.** "Social persuasion may entail encouragement or specific performance feedback from a supervisor or a colleague or it may involve discussions in the teachers' lounge, community, or media about the ability of teachers to influence students" (Goddard et al., 2004, p. 6). Once again, just as with vicarious experiences, this feedback (or discussion) only has an impact when the person from whom we're hearing it has credibility to us.

**Affective states.** "The level of arousal, either of anxiety or excitement, adds to individuals' perceptions of self-capability or incompetence. We postulate that, just as individuals react to stress, so do organizations" (Goddard et al., 2004, p. 6). If members of the group are stressed and do not feel as though there is a "light at the end of the tunnel" as far as that stress is concerned, they will have less faith in their collective ability to bring about changes. One more important aspect to this is that Goddard et al. state, "Organizations with strong beliefs in group capability can tolerate pressure and crises and continue to function without debilitating consequences" (2004, p. 6).

---

**Mindful Moment**

As you read in our discussion of the four experiences that impact efficacy, credibility is important. Teachers are tired of being a part of groups where they are told what to do and not given a voice. Those groupings lack credibility. Reflect on how you assure teachers that your collective groups are places where everyone can learn from one another and that each voice matters. Is there something more you could be doing to back this assurance up?

---

## WHY DO WE NEED COLLECTIVE TEACHER EFFICACY?

Throughout this book, I have highlighted numerous reasons why leadership is difficult and why we cannot go it alone in any leadership position. We need to work collaboratively with others to address our greatest needs. We can let needs like budget cuts, school consolidations, and poor morale put us in crisis mode, or we can try to build collective efficacy when we want to improve our grading practices, incorporate more effective feedback into student learning, or create trauma-informed practices for students so that they are more engaged in learning. Collective efficacy can be fostered around any issue we are facing in school.

The reasoning behind that thought is simple; when a diverse group of people put their thoughts together in supportive conditions and do their best thinking while they are doing that collaborative work, it gives us the power to achieve any goal we set for ourselves in a school.

Collective teacher efficacy is meant to motivate teachers to do their very best. If teachers feel motivated, they will deepen their practices, work in collaboration with one another, and provide feedback to each other. Motivation is meant to provide teachers with agency, where they feel like they have a valued voice in their profession. However, there is a bit of a catch. Leithwood and Mascall (2008) suggest that there are two areas that impact motivation and agency, which are capacity beliefs and context beliefs. Leithwood and Mascall explain that "capacity beliefs include such psychological states as self-efficacy, self-confidence, academic self-concept, and aspects of self-esteem" (p. 535).

Context beliefs suggest that "the working conditions in the school will support teachers' efforts to instruct in the manner suggested by the school's improvement initiatives" (p. 536). It's not enough that leaders demand teachers work together because it builds collective efficacy. Leaders must set up the dynamic in which teachers feel supported in the work that they do.

I'm not just saying that because it sounds good. I'm saying that because I have experienced it as a principal.

When I was a principal, our school district suffered budget cuts, and as a result it had to close one of the smaller schools. The school that I led had to absorb the whole student population of that school. It was a hard time in our district, but our staff came together, even with a parent who was writing a community-wide hate blog. Not only did we make the consolidation work, after a yearlong process, we had also successfully brought together two fractured communities and created a new whole.

As another example, during a heightened time of accountability and mandates, staff morale was at a low, and it was having a negative impact on our school community. At a meeting of our Principal's Advisory Council (PAC), which was made up of two chairs (the building union representatives) and one stakeholder from each grade level and special area, we did an activity on chart paper to flesh out what our biggest issues were. Then we started doing the work to address those issues.

I would like to use the following blog post (DeWitt, 2011) to highlight one more example of how our staff fostered collective efficacy. The topic is the schoolwide mood around state testing, and, even though I wrote this piece almost a decade ago, you will no doubt find that the pressures are the same in your schools today.

---

### No Testing Week

*"We are raising a stressed-out generation of students who are over-tested and overanalyzed."*

The other day I took some time to craft an e-mail in a Word document. I needed to take the time to make sure that I chose my words correctly. Sending the whole staff a message is something that I take seriously because once your words are out there, they can be interpreted in numerous ways. The reason for the e-mail was to communicate something that I feel strongly about. It had to do with the overuse of testing in the U.S. and the need to focus on creativity in our school.

Once a month I meet with my Principal's Advisory Council (PAC). I have two co-chairs who are teachers within the building. They are open and honest, even when they are saying things I may not want to hear. PAC is not about venting about building issues, but about meeting to discuss how we can improve our building environment. I wanted to approach PAC about having one week that is test-free. I decided to send the staff an e-mail prior to PAC because I wanted them to understand where I was coming from.

As a principal and educator, I am concerned that all we ever hear about is testing. Our scores are available on-line to anyone who wants to see them. However, our school environment is not available for everyone. The happiness and engagement levels of our students are not available either, so in the end, clicking on a link that says *"See How Your Kids Are Doing"* really means *"See how your kids are doing in one particular area that took place over a three-day period."*

I am fortunate because I work with great staff and awesome kids, but I worry that we are only measured by a test and not by our creativity. I want our kids to live and breathe creativity all the time, but I need to begin with one week. Just one week to open up new doors for them. One week without test anxiety. Perhaps we will even out-law the word **test**.

## No Testing Week

During the week of November 28 through December 2, our school is not doing any testing of any kind. We are participating in our very own "**No Testing Week**." Teachers are not going to give science tests, social studies tests, math quizzes or spelling tests. They will not be able to progress monitor. Our students are going to have a week where they do not have to worry about the pre-test at the beginning of the week or the looming exam at the end of the week.

Instead, we are focusing on doing projects and other creative activities. Our school participates in two Scholastic Book Fairs and the week that brings November and December together is one of the weeks Scholastic will be at our school. Our students will be able to buy books all week long. They will be surrounded by books all week long. They will have extra time to get lost in the wonder of their favorite book all week long. On Friday evening, December 2, we are having local children's author **Matt McElligott** come to present and read to children and families.

The reasons for doing this are plentiful. In the United States we are too focused on testing, and I strongly believe the only way to bring back creativity is for principals to give teachers permission to spend time without worrying about data. Good data that informs instruction will always be important, but I do not believe we always collect good data. I also believe we are raising a stressed-out generation of students who are over-tested and overanalyzed.

## Teacher Reaction

Teachers were ecstatic, which surprised me because I was not sure if they would be on board with spending a week without data. However, they were happy to be given free rein to focus on projects and other creative activities that are highly effective in building student engagement. I could feel the tension in the building slip away. Although our **No Testing Week** is more than a month away, we already have many great school building initiatives planned. The following are *some* of the activities we will be doing:

- Reader's theatre involving one of Matt's books
- Deb, our librarian, will be building a pit (swimming pool) in her library which is the setting of Matt's book *Uncle Frank's Pit*. Students will be filling the pit with different objects by the end of the week.
- All students and staff will be writing about their favorite book and hanging their pieces around the school.
- All three fourth-grade classes will be building a long house with their students (Social Studies curriculum). Every class will be responsible for building a section.
- I will be digitally recording myself reading books, and our librarian will set it to a PowerPoint. The PowerPoint will be made into a movie with graphics. During the day, teachers can go to the shared folder, bring up the PowerPoint and listen to me read the story.
- We will read *Bean Thirteen* and will be making mosaics.
- Teachers will be using Matt's book *The Lion's Share* to teach students measurement and fractions, which means some baking will be involved.
- All teachers will be involved in project-based learning projects with their students.
- Our school will be transformed into a creative environment for learning, which will spur more ideas.

I understand that we can do these activities regardless of testing. However, the building environment changes when there is testing involved. People are less patient and more stressed. We know testing is our reality, but for one week it will be the furthest thing from our minds.

Perhaps we will find other weeks to do this again and we will all learn to not let testing get in our way. After all, it's an elementary school, and all elementary schools should be places that spark the imagination and not put it out.

Feel free to start a testing revolution of your own, and take a break from testing.

No Testing Week was a reaction to the stress we felt when it came to testing. Together we thought of ways to alleviate that stress for our students and ourselves. I did not realize at the time I was helping to foster collective efficacy. What I knew is that we were coming together to overcome one of our biggest challenges, and this particular example of how we came together did have a positive impact on student learning.

As a consultant working with schools nationally and internationally, I have seen leaders and teachers working together to explore their greatest issues and begin doing the work to alleviate those issues and make their school climate stronger. We need collective efficacy, not because it's popular, but because it elevates the voices of the group and can help overcome the greatest issues a school is facing. Donohoo, Hattie, and Eells (2018) explain how it works: "When efficacy is present in a school culture, educators' efforts are enhanced—especially when they are faced with difficult challenges. Since expectations for success are high, teachers and leaders approach their work with an intensified persistence and strong resolve" (p. 40).

## LEADERSHIP EFFICACY

What about leaders? We know that leaders have to understand their own self-efficacy as well. In the literature, this is referred to as *leadership efficacy*, and Bandura's research helps us look deeper into that phenomenon. Bandura (2011, p. 122) found that

> [w]hen faced with obstacles, setbacks and failures, those who doubt their capabilities slacken their efforts, give up prematurely, or settle for poorer solutions. Those who have a strong **belief** in their capabilities redouble their effort to master the challenges.

Teachers do not have to have a strong sense of self-efficacy to build collective efficacy with a group. In fact, the experience of working with a group can raise a teacher's sense of self-efficacy. Why can't the same be said for leaders?

What if we took that idea of teachers working together toward a larger impact on student learning and opened it up to leaders too? Yes, leaders can be an integral part of collective teacher efficacy, by working side by side with teachers. What if we then took the idea of that collective effort and looked at just leaders? Collective teacher efficacy has been well-researched and shown to have a powerful impact on student learning. However, leaders need to learn how to work together and have an impact as well.

At the beginning of this chapter, I mentioned that leaders often limit themselves when it comes to focusing on collective efficacy. One area in which this is most likely to happen is the composition of their leadership team. Imagine how strong a building climate could be if a principal built collective leader efficacy with his or her assistant principals. Too often assistant principals are at the mercy of their leader and do not always work in conjunction with him or her. Let's take instructional leadership, for instance. If principals only allow their assistant principals to focus on discipline—and this is the case in many schools—then those assistant principals are not getting the necessary training they need to focus on instructional strategies and student engagement and will not be prepared to be instructional leaders when they get their own building role and become a principal. I understand that there are principals who do not know how to practice instructional leadership, but they can further their education in that area by working with their leadership team. As powerful as collective teacher efficacy has proven to be, principals and assistant principals must work harder together to build collective leader efficacy, which can have a positive impact on student learning as well.

Unfortunately, not all leadership teams are created equally. And when I say "leadership teams," I mean those teams consisting of a superintendent and principals; or principals and their assistant principals; or even principals, instructional coaches and teacher leaders. All of those positions are leadership positions and fall under the realm of collective leader efficacy.

Figure 6.1 illustrates how many teams function in terms of impact versus collaboration, and it provides the reasoning for collective leader efficacy. With the right people on the team, with the right focus and a supportive leader, all leadership teams can move to the upper right-hand corner.

**Low Impact/Low Collaboration.** The members of the leadership team don't meet often, and their meetings lack a true focus on learning.

**Figure 6.1**

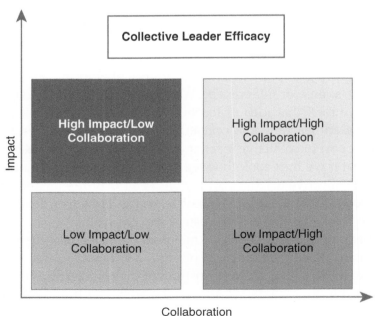

**Low Impact/High Collaboration.** The members of the leadership team meet often, but what they discuss does not have a positive impact on student learning. During the meetings they talk a lot about compliance issues and mandates, but they do not often focus on how any of their work together should impact student learning.

**High Impact/Low Collaboration.** The members of this team do not meet often or, sometimes, at all. However, they have a high impact. Don't get too excited, because high impact does not always equate to a positive impact. All the leaders on the team have individual grade levels or departments that they lead, which may lead to positive impact in those pocket areas but not the overall school community. Other times, the impact may be negative. The leaders from the team focus too much on implementation walks and compliance, and it creates a negative climate in their school community.

**High Impact/High Collaboration.** The members of the leadership team meet consistently, and their focus is always on learning. Together they build a common language and common understanding, but they also understand how to leverage each member's strengths and insights. All of this leads to a positive impact on student learning.

Too often, leaders come together and collaborate as a group but the results have little positive impact on student learning. That is *not* an example of collective leader efficacy. Collective leader efficacy, which involves the collective effort of leaders focused on learning, is equally as important as collective teacher efficacy because it involves leaders working together in their small administrative group on goals that will have a positive impact on student learning. Perhaps one of the goals involves establishing a common language and common understanding as a leadership team. Or, it may involve how leaders learn together by doing walkthroughs or formal teacher observations. The truth is, a fractured administrative team can have a negative impact on a school climate, because each individual leader may engage in negative conversations about his or her administrative colleagues in order to try to make himself or herself look better, all of which can make teachers feel unsteady about their school's leadership. Collective leader efficacy would not encourage that behavior; indeed, it would bring out quite the opposite kinds of conversations. In fact, collective leader efficacy could not only help a principal improve but also help prepare his or her assistant principals to be better principals in the future.

### How can you build collective leader efficacy?

- Ensure that each member of the leadership team contributes his or her thoughts when you are constructing a common goal.
- Decide what leaders in the group most need to know about student learning. In this book, I have tried to focus on those areas and do it at the level of building leaders or instructional coaches.

- Principals need to lower their status and help raise the status of the assistant principals on the team. This doesn't mean that principals lose their status—on the contrary, principals who lower their status in order to raise the status of assistant principals show very strong leadership.
- Decide how you can use the implementation cycle included in this book to help you begin focusing on your chosen goal.
- Collect evidence to understand impact.

---

### Mindful Moment

In your experience, do assistant principals have a strong voice in decisions around learning? Does the principal feel supported by his or her assistants, and do the assistants get the opportunity to engage in discussions focusing on learning in the classrooms?

---

## WHEN DO WE BUILD COLLECTIVE EFFICACY?

Sometimes collective teacher efficacy and collective leader efficacy are built naturally, on the spur of a moment when we realize we need to improve a situation. Other times, leaders and teachers do not need to count on a good crisis to help them build collective teacher efficacy. Schools looking to improve the learning environment for students can just as easily build collective efficacy through looking at their grading practices, creating restorative justice programs or taking time to focus on enriching the way they teach conceptual understandings to students.

Too often, school leaders wait for a crisis to build collective efficacy. And by that time, they may find it hard to build collective efficacy to help them respond to the crisis if their behavior up to that point did not always support the idea that teachers have a voice. Stakeholder groups that are really assembled just to support the idea of the leader are a hollow way to build collective efficacy. Unfortunately, when a crisis comes along it may be too late for a leader to elicit good help from teachers if those teachers never felt as though they had a voice before. To put it another way, a feeling of helplessness among teachers who feel their ideas are unwanted or their opinions go unheard can have a negative impact on the school climate: "[I]f educators' perceptions are filtered through the belief that there is very little they can do to influence student achievement, negative beliefs pervade the school culture. When educators lack a sense of collective efficacy, they do not pursue certain courses of action because they feel they or their students lack the capabilities to achieve positive outcomes" (Donohoo et al., 2018, n.p.).

**Figure 6.2**    Implementation Cycle for Instructional Leaders

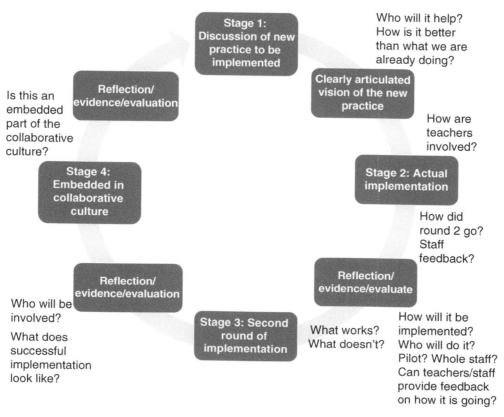

Based on research by Odom et al. (2014) and Fixsen et al. (2005).

Something else to keep in mind is that leaders often believe that they are supposed to be building collective efficacy with their whole staff. Although that may be true, and it is worth our efforts to do so, we can build collective efficacy in smaller but equally as powerful ways.

Those smaller methods of building collective efficacy, whether collective teacher efficacy or collective leader efficacy, happen when authentic professional learning communities work together on a goal they have constructed. They happen in our stakeholder groups, such as PAC, and in our grade-level groups or departments at the middle- and high-school levels.

To illustrate the development of collective efficacy, I want to bring back the implementation cycle from earlier in the book. Through this process of implementation, teachers and leaders can come together collectively, or leaders can work within their administrative team to prepare themselves for conversations with teachers and students. All of these groups learn from one another during the reflection/feedback process, which should ultimately have a positive impact on student learning. If it doesn't have a positive impact on student learning, then why spend the time doing it?

> ## Mindful Moment
>
> Take a moment to reflect on your implementation process. Does it look similar to the one in Figure 6.2? If so, do you find that slowing down the process and listening to the voices of those in the group leads to a more positive impact on student learning?

/////////////////////////////////////////////////////////////////////

## Student Voice Questions

How might you incorporate students into the implementation cycle? For example, perhaps they can provide feedback around the implementation of walkthroughs. What if they are invited to reflect with teachers on how the implementation went? What are your thoughts?

/////////////////////////////////////////////////////////////////////

## WHY IS COLLECTIVE EFFICACY HARD TO BUILD?

As you may have guessed, getting adults to come together and focus on a goal is not an easy task. Many of us, in the field of education, entered into the teaching profession because we loved working with children and young adults or we loved specific content. Perhaps we had great experiences in school as students that we wanted to continue as teachers. Or we had negative experiences in school that we wanted to prevent for the next generation of students. My point is that while most of us share a passion either for teaching children or for a particular subject, we did not enter the field of teaching to work with other adults. Working with adults can be challenging and frustrating. We are so used to controlling our domains as teachers that it's hard to let go of that control when working with other adults.

In order to work effectively with a group, we have to have a great deal of trust. This is not new information. Unfortunately, many teachers are so tired of being a part of shared-decision-making committees where they have no real shared-decision-making power that a request they join another group meeting is not always met with trust.

When it comes to collective leader efficacy, assistant principals often do not speak until the principal has given them permission to do so, because assistants believe—rightly so—that principals have more status than assistant principals. Sometimes assistant principals do not speak up because they are so inexperienced that they do not feel comfortable sharing their thoughts, for fear of being wrong. Additionally, some may not want to step outside of what they see as the typical assistant principal role of focusing on discipline, so they do not always delve into conversations about learning with their leader.

Knowing that adults do not always "trust the process," we have to make sure that we foster diverse voices in our collective meetings. This takes strong leadership. Having a voice in the process does not always mean we get our way, but it does mean that we have open dialogue around issues and that we can go into these meetings with one idea and come out with a better one. This involves the ability to challenge each other's thinking respectfully and not hold a grudge if someone gently criticizes or disagrees with our contributions.

Collective efficacy is about taking on a challenge as a team and accepting all the positive and negative experiences that can come along with that work—and then making sure we are collecting evidence of how well we are meeting that challenge.

## COLLECTIVE EFFICACY: A PROGRAM LOGIC MODEL

In order to come together and build collective teacher efficacy, leaders need to make sure teachers and staff understand why they are coming together in the first place. A few years ago, I was getting ready to run a workshop for instructional leadership teams. We were about 30 minutes from beginning when I overheard a teacher say to her colleague, "Do you know why I'm here? The principal called last night and said I needed to be here because we needed representatives from our school." It was then that I realized one of the most important parts of the process is to help people understand *why* they are a part of this collaborative team.

It sounds simple, but more times than I can count, people are asked to be a part of the group, or are "voluntold" to do so, but really have no idea why they are there. It's very difficult to build collective teacher efficacy when people do not understand why they are in the room. Below are some suggestions to help you prevent that from happening.

- Define why each member is a part of the team.
- Define the expectations of being on the team.
- Construct a common goal together around an initiative.
- Assign duties to each member of the team.
- Promote and support discourse among the members.

Donohoo et al. (2018) write: "Leaders can also influence collective efficacy by setting expectations for formal, frequent, and productive teacher collaboration and by creating high levels of trust for this collaboration to take place. 'Productive' means that teachers' collaborative efforts can help to account for consequences in the classroom" (n.p.). Trust is built one conversation and one action at a time. Trust is built when those who work in a school building feel valued.

Using the consistent theme of a program logic model, I'd like to illustrate what staff members need by setting up a scenario to show how an idea can help build collective efficacy.

Figure 6.3    Program Logic Model Example: Collective Efficacy and Grading

## Collective Efficacy and Grading

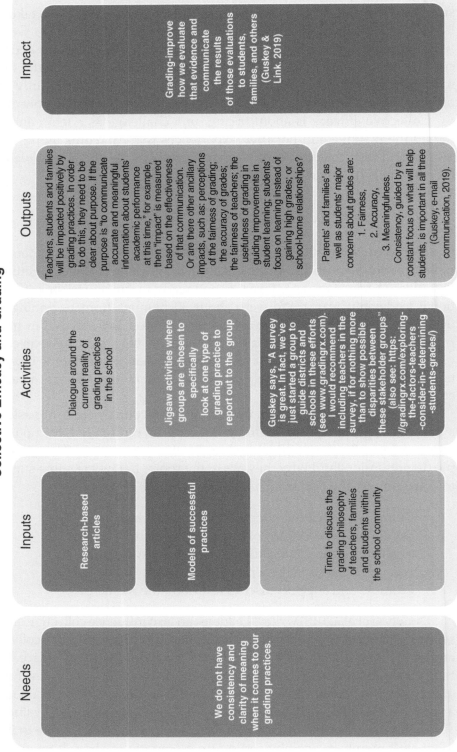

Instead of looking at a crisis situation, let's look at a situation that should be a continual focus in our schools, and that's the frequently discussed problem of grading. What we know from the work around social-emotional learning is that grading can lead to alienation of students, and yet grading practices are often too big of a problem for groups to really take time to focus on. Grading practices are worthy of our time, and they are a great place to build collective efficacy, because the decisions made by the group can have an enormous impact on student learning.

In looking at early-20th-century studies of grading, Brookhart and Guskey (2019) found that "the extent of the unreliability in grading identified in these early studies was huge. Grades for the same work varied dramatically from teacher to teacher, resulting in highly divergent conclusions about students, their learning, and their future studies" (n.p.).

Proactive measures are needed to minimize the extent of such unreliability in our own schools. According to Guskey and Link (2019), "instructional leaders at every level must give serious attention to grading and reporting" (n.p.). They suggest that principals "become familiar with the extensive knowledge base on effective grading and engage teachers in ongoing discussions about how to put this knowledge into practice." They recommend that leaders "guide their teams (including teachers, counselors, instructional coordinators, and aides) in reaching consensus about the purpose of grading and help them ensure that the policies and practices they implement are consistent, meaningful, and educationally sound." All of this offers us a perfect opportunity to combine the program logic model with collective efficacy.

Grading is a perfect academic example of how a staff can work together and build collective efficacy. A point of clarification is that I am suggesting grading practices be piloted before they are implemented schoolwide. I believe that students, parents and teachers would prefer to be able to work out issues within a smaller group as opposed to when they already involve the whole school community. Collective efficacy is about back-and-forth dialogue in which we learn from one another, and grading is a great area to focus on.

## In the End

Collective teacher efficacy is both an instructional leader's biggest area of focus and his or her biggest challenge, which makes sense: Those areas we value are not always the easiest for us to do well in, and that's what makes them so worth our time. Collective leader efficacy no doubt can be characterized similarly as difficult yet worthy. Whether we bring a group of teachers together or a group of leaders together, there is great potential to have a positive impact on student learning.

We know that there are four experiences that enhance efficacy, and we explored a few examples of how instructional leaders can build collective efficacy in their schools. One such mastery experience is defining a goal together as a staff or small group and going through the implementation cycle in Figure 6.2 to deepen the learning. It may take a while, but it could really help solidify the notion that teachers have a voice in the improvement process.

In this chapter, I wanted to explore collective efficacy as it pertains to teachers, but I also wanted to introduce you to collective leader efficacy because it is important to have on your radar. After all, collective efficacy is about forming a group, constructing a goal together around learning, and then having an impact on student learning. Collective leader efficacy is not too much of a departure from this definition; it just means getting a small group of leaders together to begin focusing on learning.

As you can tell from reading this book, all of this good advice really comes down to where we put our focus. Regardless of what our role in a school may be, the more we can talk about the different elements of learning, and the more we work through those elements with our students, the more we can have an impact on those students.

In the next, and last, chapter, we will focus on how to take all the information provided to you in this book and evaluate its impact. None of the initiatives we attempt in our schools will matter if we do not take time to evaluate their benefit to our greatest asset: our students.

## STUDY GUIDE QUESTIONS

- What does collective efficacy mean to you? Do you believe you have collective leader efficacy?
- Leithwood and Mascall researched capacity and context when it comes to motivating teachers and building agency. How do those two topics impact your leadership team?
- As a leadership team, do you involve teachers and staff in your discussions so that you can build collective efficacy?
- What do you believe is the relationship between collective efficacy and improvement of student learning?
- Before reading this chapter, did anyone in your group know that collective efficacy can be fostered among students as well as adults? If so, what examples can they provide you of how they build it in your school?
- How does your team collectively define the reasons for their inclusion and what they will individually offer to the group? Does everyone have responsibilities?
- In what ways have you used collective efficacy to implement an improvement in your school district or school board?
- What new learning did this chapter offer to you? Did it challenge your thinking in any way?

# 7

# EVIDENCE

## How Will You Evaluate Your Impact?

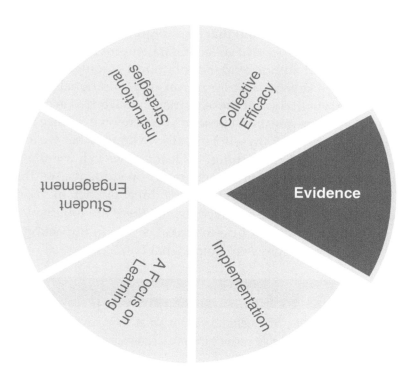

Scan this QR code for a video introduction to the chapter.

How do we know that our instructional leadership practices have an impact? How do we go from an inspiring and satisfying conversation around student learning to focusing on whether our words created actions that ultimately had an impact on it? Just as with the program logic model, we need to determine our needs, create activities that will help us meet our needs, define outputs to put the improvements into action, and then collect evidence to understand the impact of doing so. Instructional leadership is not all about our own ideas of improvement—much of it is about the ideas we inspire in others. However, we need to know that those ideas are resulting in improvements, and that is where evidence comes into our instructional leadership story.

Evidence of impact is something that is always on my mind. We often reflect on our days as leaders, but do we reflect with evidence? Without evidence, aren't we just remembering it the way we think it happened and not necessarily the way it did happen?

The interesting issue is that when I train leaders in competency-based collaborative leadership, the evidence part of the course is the most difficult but also the most rewarding. I find that leaders are good at asking teachers to collect evidence but not so good at collecting it themselves.

As a consultant and author, evidence of impact is something I often pursue. It's easy to give a keynote address or run an inspirational workshop, but it's less easy to see whether what those participants learned is actually being used in their school. The question I pose to you here on evidence of impact is the same one that I often ask myself: How do we know what we are doing is having an impact on student learning? As leaders, we can use the reasoning that we are too far removed from direct impact on students, but throughout the book I have offered ways of having more direct impact. In my role, I can use the excuse that I'm too far removed or that there are too many variables that may prevent the work that I do to make its way to impacting students, but if I don't have impact, why I am doing what I do?

### Mindful Moment

What does "evidence of impact" mean to you? In what ways have you collected evidence of your impact? If you could become the instructional leader you dream of being, where would be your greatest impact?

When looking at evidence of impact, it's all about what we are measuring, and we know we should be measuring those things we are trying to impact. I do not believe there is one specific way to measure our impact. Rather, it's about the group driving the improvement engaging in dialogue around what evidence they could collect that would show them the improvement was working. Evidence collection should not involve sitting alone in our administrative office; it should involve working collaboratively with a group.

In the competency-based work that I do, participants are required to bring evidence of impact around the six influences of collaborative leadership, which are instructional leadership, collective efficacy, professional learning and development, feedback, assessment-capable learners and family engagement.

////////////////////////////////////////////////////////////////////

## Student Voice Questions

Don't forget about the students when collecting evidence. Many participants bring in their notes or data but rarely bring in samples of students' work.

////////////////////////////////////////////////////////////////////

Additionally, when they meet to discuss their evidence, I remind them that this is not a practice of judgment, meaning that we should not judge ourselves based on the evidence we collect but look at it as a starting point. How does the evidence we collect help us understand where we are in the learning process, and what dialogue can we engage in to decide how to go further? The following image is the slide that I use when diving into the conversation regarding evidence and instructional leadership.

Collaborative dialogue is instrumental in the evidence collection process, because it helps guide us to a deeper level of learning if we choose people to collaborate with who have different ways of thinking than we do.

**Figure 7.1**   Evidence-Sharing Session

**Evidence-Sharing Session**

- **Instructional leadership**—What evidence helps support your goal of being an instructional leader?
- **Evidence sharing**
  - What evidence did you bring?
  - How did you collect it?
  - Whom did you engage in dialogue with around this evidence?
  - What did you learn?
  - What would you do differently next time?

**Time: 30 minutes**

## Evidence of Impact

In the following pages, I will guide you through the process of collecting evidence by using program logic and the implementation cycle. We will once again focus on common language and common understanding.

As I stated earlier in the book, common language and understanding are the cornerstones of a supportive and inclusive school climate. However, common language and understanding can also help build an environment around learning that I believe surpasses any discussion around content expertise.

After the program logic model has been used to bring about a common understanding of the goal, it's time to implement the cycle of learning around the goal. The implementation cycle example in Figure 7.3 specifically looks at conceptual understanding around the most commonly used words in education—words like "student engagement," "growth mindset," "differentiated instruction," "cooperative learning" and "conceptual understanding."

When going through this process, we may want to choose activities with the intent of facilitating the different levels of learning (surface, deep, and transfer), in order. For example, we can use surface-level learning by providing staff members with one research-based article around conceptual understanding that they need to read prior to a staff meeting. At the staff meeting, after discussing the research-based article, we dive into a deep level of learning by showing a video (from YouTube, from the Teaching Channel, or one created by our own teachers), and then the teacher who is the expert at the growth mindset or student engagement guides the teachers through a lesson. This is often part of what is referred to as the "flipped faculty meeting" process. Transfer-level learning comes in when teachers in the staff meeting feel inspired to try one new instructional strategy to build student engagement in the classroom, and the instructional leader sees that practice when doing walkthroughs. It is important to note that not all teachers will feel confident enough to try a new instructional strategy so quickly. They may need the additional support of an instructional coach, peer, teacher leader, or instructional leader to help them achieve the next level, that of implementing those practices in the classroom.

The evidence of impact collected, in this example, are the videos of the practice being implemented, walkthrough observation notes from the instructional leader, and the work created by the students.

Figure 7.2 Program Logic Model Example: Building Common Language and Common Understanding

## Common Language/Common Understanding

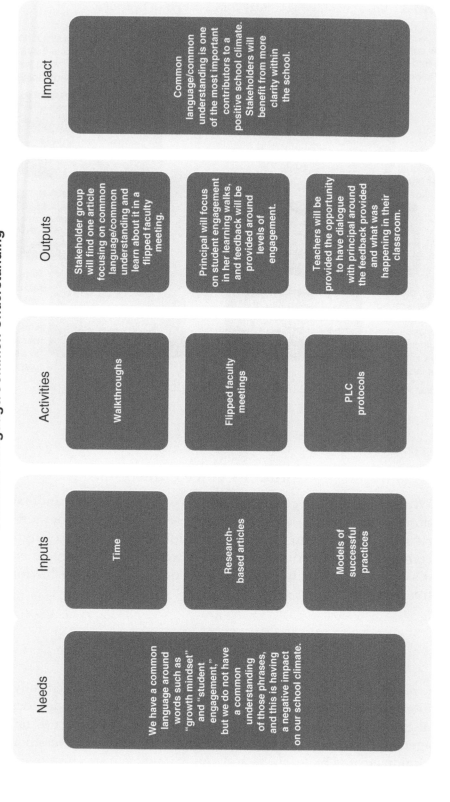

| Needs | Inputs | Activities | Outputs | Impact |
|---|---|---|---|---|
| We have a common language around words such as "growth mindset" and "student engagement," but we do not have a common understanding of those phrases, and this is having a negative impact on our school climate. | Time<br><br>Research-based articles<br><br>Models of successful practices | Walkthroughs<br><br>Flipped faculty meetings<br><br>PLC protocols | Stakeholder group will find one article focusing on common language/common understanding and learn about it in a flipped faculty meeting.<br><br>Principal will focus on student engagement in her learning walks, and feedback will be provided around levels of engagement.<br><br>Teachers will be provided the opportunity to have dialogue with principal around the feedback provided and what was happening in their classroom. | Common language/common understanding is one of the most important contributors to a positive school climate. Stakeholders will benefit from more clarity within the school. |

**Figure 7.3**    Implementation Strategy for Concepts of Learning

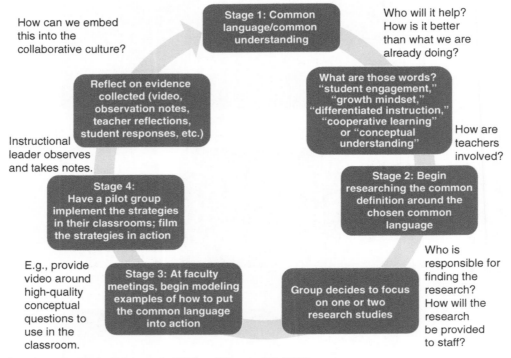

Based on research by Odom et al. (2014) and Fixsen et al. (2005).

///////////////////////////////////////////////////////////////////////

## Student Voice Questions

When it comes to common language and common understanding, don't forget the students. Randomly select students from a few classrooms, and ask them for their definition of the common language and common understanding your staff is working on. If they know it, then it's a good sign that the work you are doing with staff is having a positive impact.

///////////////////////////////////////////////////////////////////////

## STUDENT ENGAGEMENT PRACTICES

Let's move on to another example. This time we will specifically look at social-emotional learning. Figure 7.4 is a program logic model focusing on social-emotional learning, which you read about in Chapter 4, on student engagement. When I was a school principal, Kids Club was our student advisory group created by teachers, and you will notice it specifically mentioned

Figure 7.4   Program Logic Model Example: Social-Emotional Engagement

## Social-Emotional Engagement

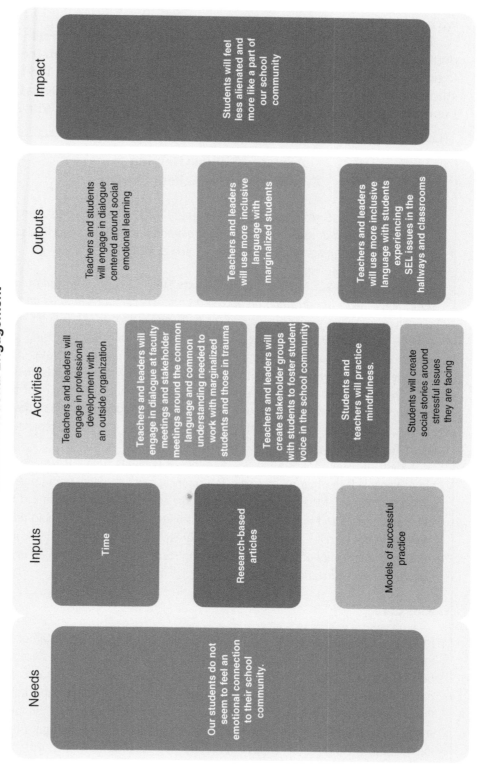

in the Outputs column. It is one of the greatest examples of student voice that we had in our school.

For those of you at the secondary level, this was actually a method of student voice that was created based on a high-school model. From the program logic model, we take a deeper look at what can be created out of it, which is a student advisory group. As I mentioned before, ours was called Kids Club, and I wrote about it for *Education Week* in the following blog post (DeWitt, 2012).

## Advisory Groups: Helping to Create a Positive School Climate

*"The Centers for Disease Control and Prevention (2009) recommends school climate reform as a data driven strategy that promotes healthy relationships, school connectedness, and dropout prevention"* (Thapa et al., 2012).

According to the latest National School Climate Study (2012), *"A growing number of State Departments of Education are focusing on school climate reform as an essential component of school improvement and/or bully prevention"* (p. 2). Schools are often looking for quality ways to create a safe atmosphere for students. Using advisory groups is one way to promote a healthier and more nurturing school climate.

Student advisory groups are not what you are probably thinking. This doesn't just mean that school social workers and school psychologists work with groups of students who are in need. Advisory groups are small groups of students that span the grades in the school system, and every staff member has a part in it. It can help make a large school feel a little bit smaller.

Student advisory groups allow for a couple of students from each grade level to get to know kids in other grade levels. It also encourages students from upper grades to be role models for the younger students in the school. Older students need to learn to be role models and understand the responsibility that comes with being the oldest students in the school. Establishing advisory groups is one way that many schools are creating a community of learners and showing students that they have an important part in their own educational process.

### Kids Club

In the school district where I am principal, we have advisory groups at all of the elementary schools. The one in our particular school has been in existence since the year before I became principal, while the other schools have created their groups over the past few years. We call our advisory group Kids Club, but one school calls their group Peace Groups, and the last school calls their advisory time together Tiger Talk (their school mascot is a tiger). Kids Club was based on an idea that our staff got from reading the book *The Big Picture: Education Is Everyone's Business* by Dennis Littky.

Advisory groups are not simple to put together, but the time it takes is well worth it when the kids meet with their advisory teacher. Typically, once or twice a month we meet with our groups for 15 minutes and talk about what is going on in the school or at home. Sometimes they complete surveys on how much they enjoy the school lunch or other aspects of the school. When I first became principal the students had an opportunity to choose which playground equipment we could get for our new playground.

The advisory group that the principal has is not all the students who frequently get into trouble. They are an evenly balanced group of students just like every other staff member has. I have about 10 students from kindergarten through fifth grade. One of the great things that happens is when a child transfers from our school to one of the other elementary schools, they understand the concept of advisory groups already and feel comfortable contributing to the group because they know the process.

### Character Education

"There is extensive research that shows school climate having a profound impact on students' mental and physical health" (Thapa et al., 2012).

I have not always been a promoter of character education programs. It's not that I don't believe in character education, because I do. I just believe that if the program doesn't become a part of the culture of a school, it is harder to see if it is effective. Advisory groups offer schools the opportunity to really delve into the topic of character education because the groups are the venue that help build the culture. In the words of Todd Whitaker, "It's people, not programs." Advisory groups will be successful if the people in the school believe in them.

In New York State we have the Dignity for All Students Act (DASA). All schools in New York State are required to *include classroom instruction that supports the development of a school environment free of discrimination and harassment, including but not limited to, instruction that raises awareness and sensitivity to discrimination and harassment based on a person's actual or perceived race, color, weight, national origin, ethnic group, religion, religious practice, disability, sexual orientation, and gender"* (N.Y. State Commissioner Regulation 100.2 (c)). Our schools are using our advisory groups as one way to meet this very important mandate.

### In the End

Advisory groups can be beneficial to creating a safe and nurturing school climate. In addition, they offer all students, even those who are new to the school, an opportunity to feel like a valued member of the educational community. Many students feel a special connection to their advisory teacher, because they may be in the same group with them for up to six years.

(Continued)

(Continued)

School culture is so important to the educational process. It's through a positive school culture that we meet the social and emotional needs of our students so they will feel safe and learn. We want our students to leave us feeling that we listened to their needs, and advisory groups are just one of the ways that schools can meet that need.

### Creating an Advisory Group:

- Three or four teachers work together with a list of all staff members.
- Add one or two students (depending on size of school) from each grade level into a group.
- Each group stays with the same staff member year after year. (This is clearly harder to do with schools that have high teacher turnover or in schools that have experienced many budget cuts.)
- Put together monthly topics that each staff member should discuss. Remember that not every staff member knows what to talk to kids about.
- Use character education words. For example, every staff member in the district is talking about "Respect" with their advisory groups.
- Each staff member should get a plastic organizer that has crayons, pencils, scissors and other supplies.
- Organization is key. School days are busy, and the more the planning group can do some of the thinking for each teacher, the better. Teachers need to be prepared on the morning or afternoon of the advisory group meeting, in the event that something comes up that morning that prevents them from having everything they need for the group.

### Advisory Groups:

- Advisory groups should last no more than 20 minutes.
- The principal or secretary uses the loudspeaker to announce the beginning and end.
- All staff members stand in the hallway to welcome students and make sure they are being polite in the hallway as they individually walk to their advisory group.
- Grades 1 through 4 students walk on their own to their Kids Club.
- Grade 5 students pick up their kindergarten Kids Club peers and walk them to their destination.
- Every Kids Club group has a plastic organizer that holds different ideas for meetings, as well as crayons, scissors, and other items needed for crafts and projects.

### References

Littky, D. (2004). *The big picture: Education is everyone's business.* Alexandria, VA: ASCD.

Thapa, A., Cohen, J., Higgins-D'Alessandro, A., & Guffey, S. (2012). *School climate research summary: August 2012.* New York, NY: National School Climate Center.

**Figure 7.5**   Implementation Strategy for Student Advisory Groups (SEL)

Based on research from Odom et al. (2014) and Fixsen et al. (2005).

Now that you have viewed the program logic model and have a deeper understanding of advisory groups, we will look at the implementation cycle used to put it into practice. This implementation cycle should happen at the very beginning of the advisory groups practice. Clearly, the cycle below will keep going on and on to reflect the growth process that the school community goes through during the advisory group process.

Something that is not reflected in the cycle or the program logic model is what I cited from Fullan's work earlier in the book around the topic of the implementation dip. When looking at social-emotional learning, student engagement, and an extra task put on teachers such as advisory groups, it's important to understand that not every staff member will be on board, and that will result in an implementation dip. Another thing to notice is the sheer amount of work that goes into planning something like advisory groups. However, the ends justify the means, because in a school community where this emotional connection to school is established among students and teachers, fewer students will feel alienated.

Over time, the evidence that can be collected will be student surveys, teacher/staff reflections, the number of discipline referrals on the days when advisory groups took place, and anecdotes around student interactions. From a surface-, deep- and transfer-level learning framework, we would look at what lessons students were learning as far as behavior was concerned, how additional lessons were incorporated into classrooms after the initial lessons learned in advisory group, and how that learning transferred to student learning when it came to students' behavior (discipline referrals, community involvement practices, etc.).

## INSTRUCTIONAL LEADERSHIP

Now that we have looked at focus on learning, student engagement, and instructional strategies (i.e., used in the focus on learning implementation example—Figure 7.3), let's end by looking at where we began, which is instructional leadership. Instructional leadership is a highly important topic and the basis of this book. Many leaders refer to themselves as instructional leaders, but many of their teachers may not agree with that. As I mentioned at the beginning of this book, in my survey of several hundred principals, nearly one fourth of the respondents affirmed that they were "very confident" in their instructional leadership ability. Another 43% stated that they were "confident" in their role as instructional leaders, and only 8% confided that they did not feel like instructional leaders at all. According to the similar survey I sent to teachers, their confidence in their principal's instructional leadership ability, on average, was much lower than the confidence the leaders themselves felt.

Why was this the case—why might teachers rate the instructional leadership ability at their school less highly than their leader does? Perhaps their leader is engaging in instructional leadership practices, but not all teachers are in close proximity of that, so they do not see the leader engaged in those behaviors. Or, it may be that many leaders believe they are instructional leaders when they really are not. So, let's take that information and incorporate it into our program logic model, as well as the implementation cycle that can be used for instructional leadership practices. Figure 7.6 gives an example of program logic where instructional leadership is concerned.

As you can see from the program logic model in Figure 7.6, the leader engages in activities and exhibits behaviors that will help him or her reach a comfortable level as far as instructional leadership is concerned. All of this is dependent on how much of a burden the leader is already under due to district office demands, accountability measures and mandates they are responsible for carrying out. Sometimes there's just too much to juggle. I want instructional leaders to understand their current reality, and use that to guide how much they can move into this instructional leadership space.

Last but not least, let's look at the implementation cycle to help show us what implementing instructional leadership practices might look like. Please remember, the implementation cycle is dependent on what you can do given your stressors. For that reason, one instructional leadership action may take only a week to complete, whereas others may take months or a year. There is no hard-and-fast rule for how long improvement may take. What we know is that it can take months or years depending on the culture and climate of the building. Although you have seen similar illustrations, the implementation cycle in Figure 7.7 focuses on walkthroughs. As mentioned in the Chapter 5 blog post on the myth of walkthroughs, it is a very popular activity among principals but is often not implemented correctly. This implementation cycle will help you make sure walkthroughs are done correctly.

In this implementation cycle I added a few more questions, and those were meant to provide an opportunity for teachers to have a voice. Walkthroughs, and instructional leadership, are about collaboration and dialogue. How can a leader and the teachers they work with learn from one another? How does the process add to the leader's level of instructional leadership?

Evidence that can be collected to understand the impact of walkthroughs includes reflection activities on the part of teachers and the leader, copies of the feedback provided by both groups, surveys completed by teachers, and evidence of how the teachers took the feedback given by the leader and used it in their instructional practices.

When looking at surface-, deep- and transfer-level learning, we can see that surface-level learning takes place when a leader and a staff member discuss the definition of walkthroughs and decide what they want out of the experience. Deep-level learning takes place when the leader begins doing the walkthroughs and provides, as well as asks, for feedback on how the activity went. Was it successful? How could it improve? Transfer-level learning happens when the leader takes that feedback and puts it into action the next time he or she completes the walkthrough process.

Figure 7.6   Program Logic Model Example: Instructional Leadership

**Instructional Leadership**

| Needs | Inputs | Activities | Outputs | Impact |
|---|---|---|---|---|
| I do not practice instructional leadership enough in my school. I spend too much time on the management side of leadership. | Research-based articles, blogs and books focusing on instructional leadership | Join an open/closed forum on social media (Twitter, Voxer, etc.) — for example, a Facebook group dedicated to instructional leadership. | Engage in one flipped faculty meeting beginning in October. | Teachers and students will engage in collaborative conversations around learning with their leader, and that leader will make sure their meetings keep a consistent focus on improvements to the learning environment. |
| | Webinars focusing on instructional leadership | Work with a leadership coach, peer, or superintendent on increasing instructional leadership practices. | Engage in walkthroughs that will help foster feedback in the school community starting in October. | |
| | Videos that help model instructional leadership practices | Collaborate with my stakeholder group and learn what they want out of an instructional leader. | Attend PLC meetings where the focus is on growth measures or instructional strategies. | |
| | Define what instructional leadership practices are most important to me | Create a survey for teachers (and student groups when age appropriate) asking what they want out of their leader. | | |

**Figure 7.7**    Implementation Strategy for Walkthroughs

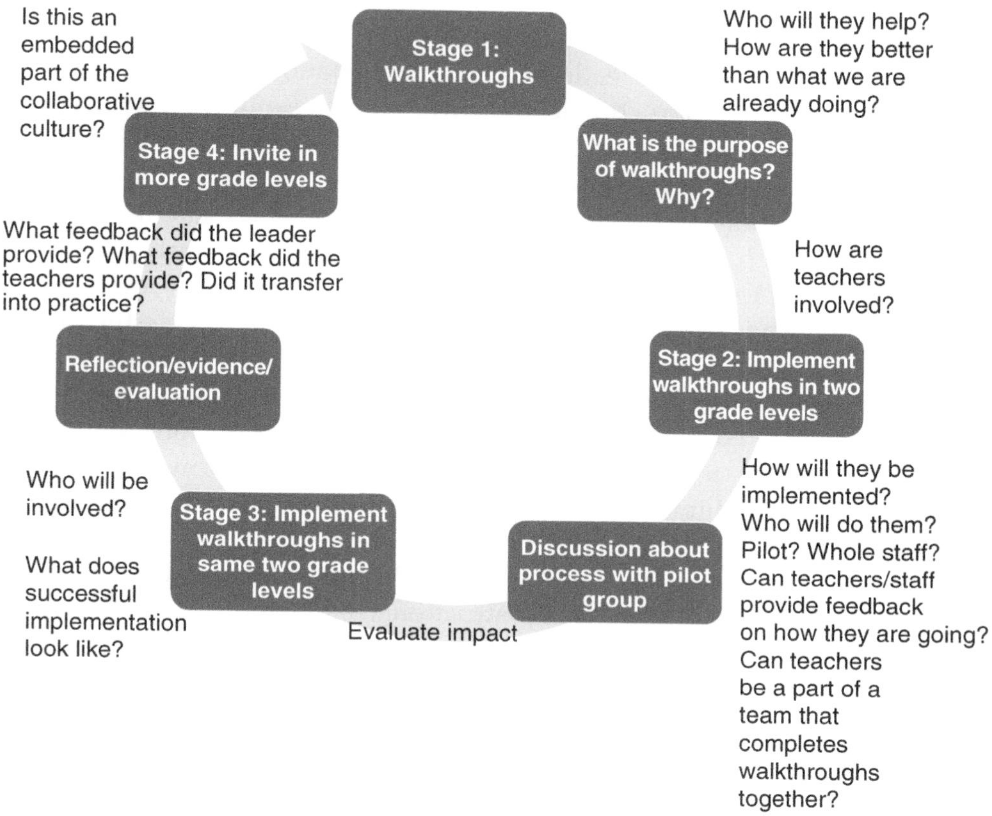

Is this an embedded part of the collaborative culture?

**Stage 1: Walkthroughs**

Who will they help? How are they better than what we are already doing?

**Stage 4: Invite in more grade levels**

**What is the purpose of walkthroughs? Why?**

What feedback did the leader provide? What feedback did the teachers provide? Did it transfer into practice?

How are teachers involved?

**Reflection/evidence/ evaluation**

**Stage 2: Implement walkthroughs in two grade levels**

Who will be involved?

What does successful implementation look like?

**Stage 3: Implement walkthroughs in same two grade levels**

Evaluate impact

**Discussion about process with pilot group**

How will they be implemented? Who will do them? Pilot? Whole staff? Can teachers/staff provide feedback on how they are going? Can teachers be a part of a team that completes walkthroughs together?

Based on research by Odom et al. (2014) and Fixsen et al. (2005).

## IN THE END

As I stated before, there is no hard-and-fast rule for how long implementation takes. However, I can tell you it's never as fast as we want it to be, and we often have to spend more time on it than we expect to. That's why it is so important to take one area and focus on it. Any other way of approaching improvement will probably fail because we didn't take enough time to collaborate with staff and dive deep into what it looks like, as well as discuss how to learn from those moments it does not go well.

It is my hope that in this chapter I have provided you with enough explanation of how to understand our impact by engaging in activities and collecting evidence to see what was successful and what was not. In order to be instructional leaders, we have to put learning at the heart of what we do, and we have to make ourselves vulnerable enough that it is okay for us to make mistakes in front of our staff.

Instructional leadership is when those in a leadership position focus their efforts on the implementation of practices that will increase student learning. Throughout the book I have focused on six components that I believe are central to instructional leadership: implementation, focus on learning, student engagement, instructional strategies, collective efficacy and evidence of impact. These are six practical ways that leaders can practice instructional leadership and have a positive impact on student learning.

This information is based on my experience as a school principal and on research I have engaged in for decades, particularly my deep research of the topic over the last year. It is also based on what I have learned by working with some of the leading educational experts in the world, and the information has come from what I have learned by working with thousands of leaders, teachers, specialists and instructional coaches over the last five years as a consultant and author. I would like to leave you with one last piece of information. It is an instructional leadership framework that I created while writing this book. It is not meant to be a judgment of your present abilities, but it is meant to provide you with a starting point. Please reflect on, and decide where you sit presently in, all of these parts of instructional leadership. Out of the many different components, where would you start digging in first? Would you choose an area where you already have confidence but want to go deeper, or one that represents an area of growth for you?

Instructional leadership is the most researched form of leadership but the most difficult to display. Researchers can tell us where we should focus our time, but many of those researchers do not have a leadership background, so please just keep that in mind as you move forward. Try to find a balance between what they advise and what you can realistically do. That even goes for what I wrote in this book. Find a place in all of these instructional leadership practices, and begin with the one that makes the most sense for you.

As always, thank you for taking the time to read this book. I hope you enjoyed learning from it as much as I learned from writing it.

# Reflection Tool

| Influence | Beginning | Emerging | Proficient | Excellent |
|---|---|---|---|---|
| Implementation | Leader understands that the use of an implementation cycle may be beneficial to implementing improvements in the school but creates one without teacher input. | Leader understands that the use of an implementation cycle is vitally important to implementing improvements. The leader engages in creating a cycle with teachers. | Leader engages in dialogue with teachers to create a program logic model. They use the program logic model to help them create an implementation cycle. They go through the implementation cycle once and collect evidence to help them understand impact. However, they do not use that evidence to guide new learning around the improvement. | Leader sets a clear, practical and impactful vision for quality instruction with teachers. The leader engages in dialogue with teachers to create a program logic model together. They use the program logic model to help them create an implementation cycle. They go through the implementation cycle once and collect evidence to help them understand impact. They use that evidence to help guide them through the process of making additional improvements. |
| Notes | | | | |

121

| Influence | Beginning | Emerging | Proficient | Excellent |
|---|---|---|---|---|
| **Instructional Strategies** | *Leader understands that the use of a variety of instructional strategies in the classroom is necessary to engage students. However, the leader does not have an understanding regarding the nuances of putting those strategies into practice.* | *Leader understands that the use of a variety of instructional strategies in the classroom is necessary to engage students. The leader can offer one of several strategies to use in the classroom but does not necessarily want to model them for the teacher.* | *Leader engages in dialogue with teachers that focus on different instructional strategies, which provides an opportunity to set a clear, practical and impactful vision of instructional leadership. These strategies are part of the focus of faculty meetings, PLCs or department meetings, and the leader offers samples of research to support the use of those strategies. The next step is for the leader to consistently focus with teachers on evidence of impact.* | *Leader collaboratively sets a clear, practical and impactful vision for quality instruction with teachers, using a program logic model. The leader engages in dialogue with teachers at faculty meetings, PLCs or department meetings around different instructional strategies to use in the classroom to meet the needs of students. Those strategies are offered with background research, and there are opportunities to see those strategies modeled through peer classroom observations or the use of videos that help model the lesson. Additionally, instructional strategies mentioned are used with students, and evidence is collected to understand their impact.* |
| *Notes* | | | | |

| Student Engagement | Leader does walkthroughs and formal teacher observations where student engagement is a focus. However, the leader does not ask students questions to gauge student understanding. | Leader does walkthroughs and formal teacher observations in which student engagement is a focus. The leader sits down and asks individual students questions to gauge student understanding. | Leader does walkthroughs and formal teacher observations in which academic and social-emotional student engagement is a focus. The leader creates a program logic model with teachers that may help students feel less alienated and more engaged. They also use an implementation cycle to help build a common language and common understanding around that student engagement area of focus. | Leader engages in a program logic model with teachers to discuss areas of need when it comes to student engagement. The leader does walkthroughs and formal teacher observations in which academic and social-emotional student engagement is a focus. The leader uses the program logic model with teachers to define ways of helping students feel less alienated and more engaged. They also use an implementation cycle to construct a common language and common understanding around that student engagement area of focus, and they collect evidence to understand impact. |
|---|---|---|---|---|
| Notes | | | | |

| Influence | Beginning | Emerging | Proficient | Excellent |
|---|---|---|---|---|
| **Focus on Learning** | *Leader sits in the back of the classroom during formal observations and does not speak with students. The leader takes notes focusing on learning intentions that are addressed by the teacher. The leader understands what the learning intentions for the class may be because there is an expectation that teachers will have them visible for students during class.* | *Leader understands that there needs to be a balance between knowledge and skills taught in the classroom. The leader will occasionally ask teacher for further details about the focus on learning taking place in class and ask teachers to explain how their instructional practices help build both knowledge and skills.* | *The leader works collaboratively with teachers to gain a better understanding of knowledge dimensions and the need for surface-, deep- and transfer-level learning. They take that learning and work together to create an implementation cycle to help them focus on one of those areas.* | *The leader works collaboratively with teachers to gain a better understanding of knowledge dimensions, conceptual understanding and the need for surface-, deep- and transfer-level learning. They take that learning and work together to create an implementation cycle to help them focus on one of those areas. The team members work together to collect evidence to understand the impact their combined thinking is having on student learning.* |
| *Notes* | | | | |

| | | | | |
|---|---|---|---|---|
| **Collective Teacher Efficacy (CTE)** | Teachers mostly work in silos. However, if teachers want to work in groups, that is fine as well. The leader appreciates that teachers will work cooperatively but does not necessarily need to see the evidence that it's working. | Teachers can either work in silos or work in cooperative grade level, PLC or department-specific groups. It all depends on what the leader wants, any of the work being done needs to follow district mandates, and teachers must provide evidence that what they are doing is working. | Leaders, as well as teacher leaders and coaches, have a deep understanding of teaching and learning. Teachers feel comfortable challenging each other's thinking and learning from that level of challenge. The group members have constructed a goal together and are beginning to collect evidence to see if their effort is working, but they are not necessarily consistent in doing so. | Each collaborative group (i.e., PLC, grade level, department, faculty) has a strong belief in each other. Together, they construct a goal that is deeply focused on a challenge they are facing (e.g., school consolidation, student learning, achievement gap). Teachers feel comfortable challenging each other's thinking and learning from that level of challenge. The group members work together and consistently try new strategies they learned from each other to meet that challenge, and they collect evidence to see if their efforts are working. The leader can provide evidence of impact when it comes to CTE. |
| *Notes* | | | | |

| Influence | Beginning | Emerging | Proficient | Excellent |
|---|---|---|---|---|
| Evidence of Impact | Leader rarely collects evidence to understand how his or her leadership actions are helping to change the school climate. However, it is on the leader's radar and is something he or she would like to begin doing. | Leader understands the need to collect evidence around the things he or she is trying to change in the school. The leader randomly collects evidence around the changes he or she values and feel like he or she controls. The evidence collected is usually mostly anecdotal notes from teachers. | Leader works with teachers to engage in collaborative dialogue around what needs to be improved in the school community. The leader readily pays attention to the needs of students and teachers and engages in program logic to define the improvements needed, as well as the necessary actions to achieve those improvements. The leader engages in implementation cycles and goes through the learning process encouraged by collecting evidence during those cycles. However, he or she does not consistently use that evidence to help him or her improve. | Leader works with teachers to engage in collaborative dialogue around what needs to be improved in the school community. The leader readily pays attention to the needs of students and teachers and engages in program logic to define the improvements needed, as well as the necessary actions to achieve those improvements. The leader engages in implementation cycles, goes through the learning process encouraged by collecting evidence during those cycles, and consistently uses that evidence to improve his or her practice. |
| Notes | | | | |

# Study Guide Questions

- How often does your group come together around an influence on learning and share evidence that each of you have collected?

- What evidence do you collect to understand your individual impacts as instructional leaders?

- In your district or school board, will you use the program logic model when implementing a new improvement?

- What is the relationship between what you learned individually, and as a group, in this chapter and what you presently do in your roles?

- If your teachers were surveyed about your level of instructional leadership, how do you think they might answer?

- How will the reflection sheet help guide you in your instructional leadership practices? How might you use it as a team? How might you use it as an individual?

# References

Anderson, L. W. & Krathwohl, D. R. (Eds.). (2001a). *A taxonomy for learning, teaching, and assessing: A revision of Bloom's Taxonomy of Educational Objectives* (Complete edition). New York, NY: Longman.

Anderson, L. W., & Krathwohl, D. R. (Eds.). (2001b). *A taxonomy for learning, teaching, and assessing: A revision of Bloom's Taxonomy of Educational Objectives* (1st ed. Abridged). New York, NY: Pearson.

The Australian Society for Evidence Based Teaching. (n.d.). *Nurturing deep learning*. Retrieved March 20, 2019, from http://www.evidencebasedteaching.org.au

Bandura, A. (1977). Self-efficacy: Toward a unifying theory of behavioral change. *Psychological Review, 84,* 191–215.

Bandura, A. (1986). *Social foundations of thought and action: A social cognitive theory*. Englewood Cliffs, NJ: Prentice Hall.

Bandura, A. (2000). Cultivate self-efficacy for personal and organizational effectiveness. In E. A. Locke (Ed.), *Handbook of principles of organizational behavior* (pp. 9–35). New York, NY: Oxford University Press.

Bandura, A. (2011). Cultivate self-efficacy for personal and organizational effectiveness. In E. A. Locke (Ed.), *The handbook of principles of organizational behavior: Indispensable knowledge for evidence-based management* (2nd ed., pp. 120–136.), New York, NY: Oxford University Press.

Bartlett, J. D., Smith, S., & Bringewatt, E. (2017). *Helping young children who have experienced trauma: Policies and strategies for early care and education*. New York, NY: National Center for Children in Poverty, Columbia University. http://www.nccp.org/publications/pdf/text_1180.pdf

Biggs, J., & Tang, C. (2007). *Teaching for quality learning at university: What the student does* (3rd ed.). Buckingham, UK: Open University Press.

Bloom, B. S. (Ed.). (1956). *Taxonomy of educational objectives: The classification of educational goals*. New York, NY: D. McKay & Co.

Brookhart, S. M., & Guskey, T. R. (2019, May). Are grades reliable? Lessons from a century of research. *ASCD Education Update, 61*(5). Retrieved from http://www.ascd.org/publications/newsletters/education-update/may19/vol61/num05/Are-Grades-Reliable%C2%A2-Lessons-from-a-Century-of-Research.aspx

Burns, M. (2019, February 19). I'm a neuroscientist. Here's how teachers change kids' brains. *EdSurge.* https://www.edsurge.com/news/2019-02-19-i-m-a -neuroscientist-here-s-how-teachers-change-kids-brains

Bush, A. J., Kennedy, J. J., & Cruickshank, D. R. (1977). An empirical investigation of teacher clarity. *Journal of Teacher Education, 28*(2), 53–58. https://doi.org/10.1177 /002248717702800216

Centre for Innovation and Excellence in Learning, Vancouver Island University. (n.d.). *Ten metacognitive teaching strategies.* Nanaimo, BC, Canada: Author. Retrieved April 9, 2019, from https://ciel.viu.ca/teaching-learning-pedagogy /designing-your-course/how-learning-works/ten-metacognitive-teaching -strategies

Chief Council of State School Officials (CCSSO). (2015). *Interstate School Leaders Licensure Consortium's (ISLLC) standards for school leaders.* Retrieved February 13, 2019, from https://ccsso.org/resource-library/professional-standards-educational -leaders

Claxton, G. (2007). Expanding young people's capacity to learn. *British Journal of Educational Studies, 55*(2), 115–134. doi:10.1111/j.1467-8527.2007.00369.x

Coates, H. (2005). The value of student engagement for higher education quality assurance. *Quality in Higher Education, 11* (1), 25–36.

Coates, H. (2009). *Engaging students for success: Australasian student engagement report—Australasian Survey of Student Engagement.* Victoria, Australia: Australian Council for Educational Research. https://research.acer.edu.au/cgi /viewcontent.cgi?article=1017&context=higher_education

Collaborative for Academic, Social, and Emotional Learning. (2013a). *CASEL schoolkit: A guide for implementing schoolwide academic, social, and emotional learning.* Chicago, IL: Author.

Collaborative for Academic, Social, and Emotional Learning. (2013b). *2013 CASEL guide: Effective social and emotional learning programs—Preschool and elementary school edition.* Chicago, IL: Author.

Day, C., Gu, Q., & Sammons, P. (2016). The impact of leadership on student outcomes: How successful school leaders use transformational and instructional strategies to make a difference. *Educational Administration Quarterly, 52*(2), 221–258. https://doi.org/10.1177/0013161X15616863

DeWitt, P. (2011, October 7). No testing week. *Peter DeWitt's Finding Common Ground* [blog]. *Education Week.* Retrieved from http://blogs.edweek.org/edweek /finding_common_ground/2011/10/no_testing_week.html

DeWitt, P. (2012, September 25). Advisory groups: Creating a positive school community. *Peter DeWitt's Finding Common Ground* [blog]. *Education Week.* Retrieved from http://blogs.edweek.org/edweek/finding_common_ground/2012/09 /advisory_groups_creating_a_positive_school_community.html

DeWitt, P. (2014a, August 24). Help! My principal says he's an instructional leader! *Peter DeWitt's Finding Common Ground* [blog]. *Education Week.* Retrieved from http://blogs.edweek.org/edweek/finding_common_ground/2014/08/help _my_principal_says_hes_an_instructional_leader.html

DeWitt, P. (2014b, November 9). Four obstacles to implementation. *Peter DeWitt's Finding Common Ground* [blog]. *Education Week*. Retrieved from http://blogs.edweek.org/edweek/finding_common_ground/2014/11/4_obstacles_to_implementation.html

DeWitt, P. (2016a). *Collaborative leadership: Six influences that matter most*. Thousand Oaks, CA: Corwin Press.

DeWitt, P. (2016b, April 19). The myth of walkthroughs: Eight unobserved practices in schools. *Peter DeWitt's Finding Common Ground* [blog]. *Education Week*. Retrieved from https://blogs.edweek.org/edweek/finding_common_ground/2016/04/the_myth_of_walkthroughs_8_unobserved_practices_in_classrooms.html

DeWitt, P. (2017). *School climate: Leading with collective efficacy*. Thousand Oaks, CA: Corwin Press.

DeWitt, P. (2018a). *Coach it further: Using the art of coaching to improve school leadership*. Thousand Oaks, CA: Corwin Press.

DeWitt, P. (2018b). Educators need mindfulness. Their mental health may depend on it. *Peter DeWitt's Finding Common Ground* [blog]. *Education Week*. Retrieved from http://blogs.edweek.org/edweek/finding_common_ground/2018/08/educators_need_mindfulness_their_mental_health_may_depend_on_it.html

DeWitt, P. (2019, January 20). Four reasons educators use research and four reasons they don't. *Peter DeWitt's Finding Common Ground* [blog]. *Education Week*. Retrieved from https://blogs.edweek.org/edweek/finding_common_ground/2019/01/4_reasons_educators_use_research_and_4_reasons_they_dont.html

DiNapoli, P. P. (2016). Implementation science: A framework for integrating evidence-based practice. *American Nurse Today, 11*, 40–41.

Donohoo, J., Hattie, J., & Eells, R. (2018, March). The power of collective efficacy. *Educational Leadership, 75*(6, "Leading the Energized School"), 40–44. Retrieved from http://www.ascd.org/publications/educational-leadership/mar18/vol75/num06/The-Power-of-Collective-Efficacy.aspx

Edmonds, R. (1979). Effective schools for the urban poor. *Educational Leadership, 37*, 15–24.

Education Week Research Center. (2014). *Engaging students for success: Findings from a national survey*. Bethesda, MD: Author. https://secure.edweek.org/media/ewrc_engagingstudents_2014.pdf

Elmore, R. F. (2000). *Building a new structure for school leadership*. Washington, DC: Albert Shanker Institute. http://www.shankerinstitute.org/sites/shanker/files/building.pdf

Erickson, H. L. (2008). *Stirring the head, heart, and soul: Redefining curriculum, instruction and concept-based learning*. Thousand Oaks, CA: Corwin Press.

Fendick, F. (1990). The correlation between teacher clarity of communication and student achievement gain: A meta-analysis. (PhD dissertation). Gainesville: University of Florida.

Fixsen, D. L., Naoom, S. F., Blasé, K. A., Friedman, R. M., & Wallace, F. (2005). *Implementation research: A synthesis of the literature*. Tampa: University of South Florida, National Implementation Research Network.

Flavell, J. H. (1979). Metacognition and cognitive monitoring: A new area of cognitive–developmental inquiry. *American Psychologist, 34*(10), 906–911. http://dx.doi.org/10.1037/0003-066X.34.10.906

Fredricks, J. A., Blumenfeld, P. C., & Paris, A. H. (2004). School engagement: Potential of the concept, state of the evidence. *Review of Educational Research, 74* (1), 59–109.

Fullan, M. (2007). *Leading in a culture of change.* San Francisco, CA: Jossey-Bass.

Fullan, M. (2019). *Nuance: Why some leaders succeed and others fail.* Thousand Oaks, CA: Corwin Press.

Fullan, M., & Quinn, J. (2016). *Coherence: The right drivers in action for schools, districts, and systems.* Thousand Oaks, CA: Corwin Press; Ontario, CA: Ontario Principals' Council.

Fuller, E. J., Young, M. D., Richardson, M. S., Pendola, A., & Winn, K. M. (2018). The pre-K–8 school leader: A 10-year study. Alexandria, VA: National Association of Elementary School Principals. https://www.naesp.org/sites/default/files/NAESP%2010-YEAR%20REPORT_2018.pdf

Glasgow Centre for Population Health. (2018). *Family and child poverty.* Retrieved from https://www.gcph.co.uk/children_and_families/family_and_child_poverty

Goddard, R., Hoy, W. K., & Hoy, A. W. (2004). Collective efficacy beliefs: Theoretical developments, empirical evidence, and future directions. *Educational Researcher, 33*(3), 3–13. https://doi.org/10.3102%2F0013189X033003003

Gonzalez, J. (2015, October 15). The big list of class discussion strategies. *Cult of Pedagogy* [blog]. Retrieved April 9, 2019, from https://www.cultofpedagogy.com/speaking-listening-techniques/

Guskey, T. R., & Brookhart, S. M. (Eds.). (2019). *What we know about grading: What works, what doesn't, and what's next?* Alexandria, VA: ASCD.

Guskey, T. R., & Link, L. J. (2019, March). The forgotten element of instructional leadership: Grading. *Educational Leadership, 76*(6). Retrieved from http://www.ascd.org/publications/educational-leadership/mar19/vol76/num06/The-Forgotten-Element-of-Instructional-Leadership@-Grading.aspx

Hallinger, P. (2005). Instructional leadership and the school principal: A passing fancy that refuses to fade away. *Leadership and Policy in Schools, 4*, 1–20.

Hallinger, P., & Heck, R. (1996). The principal's role in school effectiveness: A review of methodological issues, 1980–1995. In K. Leithwood, J. Chapman, D. Corson, P. Hallinger, & A. Hart (Eds.), *International handbook of educational leadership and administration* (pp. 723–784). Kluwer International Handbooks of Education, Vol. 1. Dordrecht, the Netherlands: Springer.

Hargreaves, A., & Fink, D. (2006). Redistributed leadership for sustainable professional learning communities. *Journal of School Leadership, 16*(5), 550–565. https://doi.org/10.1177/105268460601600507

Hattie, J. (2012). *Visible Learning for teachers: Maximizing impact on learning.* London, England: Routledge.

Hattie, J. (2015). *What doesn't work in education: The politics of distraction.* London, UK: Pearson. https://visible-learning.org/wp-content/uploads/2015/06/John-Hattie-Visible-Learning-creative-commons-book-free-PDF-download-What-doesn-t-work-in-education_the-politics-of-distraction-pearson-2015.pdf

Hattie, J., & Donoghue, G. (2016). Learning strategies: A synthesis and conceptual model. *NPJ Science of Learning, 1*. doi:10.1038/npjscilearn.2016.13

Hattie, J., & Yates, G. (2014). *Visible Learning and the science of how we learn*. New York, NY: Routledge.

King's College London. (2019, February 22). *Troubling extent of trauma and PTSD in young people*. Retrieved from https://www.kcl.ac.uk/news/troubling-extent-of -trauma-and-ptsd-in-young-people

Koball, H., & Jiang, Y. (2018). *Basic facts about low-income children: Children under 18 years, 2016*. New York, NY: National Center for Children in Poverty, Columbia University. http://www.nccp.org/publications/pdf/text_1194.pdf

Krishnamurti, J. (n.d.). Introduction (*Life Ahead*). Retrieved March 10, 2019, from https://jkrishnamurti.org/content/introduction

Krüger, M. L., Witziers, B., & Sleegers, P. (2007). The impact of school leadership on school level factors: Validation of a causal model. *School Effectiveness and School Improvement, 18*(1), 1–20. doi:10.1080/09243450600797638

Leithwood, K., Louis, K. S., Anderson, S., & Wahlstrom, K. (2004). *Review of research: How leadership influences student learning*. New York, NY: The Wallace Foundation.

Leithwood, K., & Mascall, B. (2008, October). Collective leadership effects on student achievement. *Educational Administration Quarterly, 44*(4), 529–561.

Louis, K. S., Leithwood, K., Wahlstrom, K., & Anderson, S. (2010). *Learning from leadership: Investigating the links to improved student learning*. New York: The Wallace Foundation.

Mau, R. Y. (1989). Student alienation in a school context. *Research in Education, 42*(1), 17–28.

Odetola, T. O., Erickson, E. L., Bryan, C. E., & Walker, L. (1972). Organizational structure and student alienation. *Educational Administration Quarterly, 8*(1), 15–26.

Odom, S. L., Duda, M. A., Kucharczyk, S., Cox, A. W., & Stabel, A. (2014). Applying an implementation science framework for adoption of a comprehensive program for high school students with autism spectrum disorder. *Remedial and Special Education, 35*(2), 123–132.

Quaglia, R. J. (2016). *School voice report 2016*. N.p.: Quaglia Institute for School Voice and Aspirations. In partnership with the Quaglia Institute for Student Aspirations, Teacher Voice and Aspirations International Center, and Corwin Press. http://quagliainstitute.org/dmsView/School_Voice_Report_2016

Ratcliffe, C. (2015). *Childhood poverty and adult success*. Washington, DC: Urban Institute. https://www.urban.org/sites/default/files/publication/65766/2000369 -Child-Poverty-and-Adult-Success.pdf

Rigby, J. (2014). Three logistics of instructional leadership. *Educational Administration Quarterly, 50*(4), 610–644.

Robinson, V. M. J. (2010). From instructional leadership to leadership capabilities: Empirical findings and methodological challenges. *Leadership and Policy in Schools, 9*(1), 1–26. doi:10.1080/15700760903026748

Robinson, V. M. J., Lloyd, C. A., & Rowe, K. J. (2008). The impact of leadership on student outcomes: An analysis of differential effects of leadership types. *Educational Administration Quarterly, 44*, 635–674.

Salo, P., Nylund, J., & Stjernstrøm, E. (2015). On the practice architectures of instructional leadership. *Educational Management Administration and Leadership, 43*(4), 490–506.

Smith Family. (2018, June 21). Disadvantaged Australian children are three years behind in school. Here's how you can help. *The New Daily.* Retrieved from https://thenewdaily.com.au/sponsored/2018/06/21/australian-children-poverty-line

Social Metrics Commission. (2018). *A new measure of poverty for the UK: The final report of the Social Metrics Commission.* London, England: Author. https://socialmetricscommission.org.uk/MEASURING-POVERTY-FULL_REPORT.pdf

Southworth, G. (2002). Instructional Leadership in Schools: Reflections and empirical evidence. *School Leadership and Management, 22*(1), 73–91.

Stern, J., Lauriault, N., & Ferraro, K. (2018). *Tools for teaching conceptual understanding, elementary: Harnessing natural curiosity for learning that transfers.* Thousand Oaks, CA: Corwin Press.

Tobin, M. (2016, July). Childhood trauma: Developmental pathways and implications for the classroom. *Changing Minds: Discussions in Neuroscience, Psychology and Education,* no. 3, 1–17. https://research.acer.edu.au/cgi/viewcontent.cgi?article=1019&context=learning_processes

Trowler, V. (2010). *Student engagement: A literature review.* Heslington, York, England: The Higher Education Academy. https://www.heacademy.ac.uk/system/files/StudentEngagementLiteratureReview_1.pdf

Tschannen-Moran, M. & Barr, M. (2004). Fostering student learning: The relationship of collective teacher efficacy and student achievement. *Leadership and Policy in Schools, 3*(3), 189–209.

Tschannen-Moran, M., & Gareis, C. R. (2004). Principals' sense of efficacy: Assessing a promising construct. *Journal of Educational Administration, 42,* 573–585.

Weissberg, R. P., & Cascarino, J. (2013). Academic learning + social-emotional learning = national priority. *Phi Delta Kappan, 95*(2), 8–13. https://doi.org/10.1177/003172171309500203

Wilcox, G., McQuay, J., Blackstaffe, A., Perry, R., & Hawe, P. (2018). Supporting academic engagement in boys and girls. *Canadian Journal of School Psychology, 33*(3), 179–192. https://doi.org/10.1177/0829573517703239

Witherspoon, M., Sykes, G., & Bell, C. (2016). *Leading a classroom discussion: Definition, supporting evidence, and measurement of the ETS® National Observational Teaching Examination (NOTE) Assessment Series.* Princeton, NJ: Educational Testing Service. https://www.ets.org/Media/Research/pdf/RM-16-09.pdf

# Index

CORWIN
A SAGE Publishing Company

# *Leadership* That Makes an Impact

**LYN SHARRATT**

Explore 14 essential parameters to guide system and school leaders toward building powerful collaborative learning cultures.

**MICHAEL FULLAN**

How do you break the cycle of surface-level change to tackle complex challenges? *Nuance* is the answer.

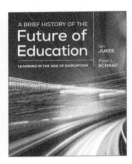

**IAN JUKES & RYAN L. SCHAAF**

The digital environment has radically changed how students need to learn. Get ready to be challenged to accommodate today's learners.

**ERIC SHENINGER**

Lead for efficacy in these disruptive times! Cultivating school culture focused on the achievement of students while anticipating change is imperative.

**JOANNE MCEACHEN & MATTHEW KANE**

Getting at the heart of what matters for students is key to deeper learning that connects with their lives.

**LEE G. BOLMAN & TERRENCE E. DEAL**

Sometimes all it takes to solve a problem is to reframe it by listening to wise advice from a trusted mentor.

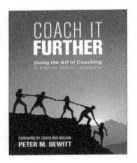

**PETER M. DEWITT**

This go-to guide is written for coaches, leaders looking to be coached, and leaders interested in coaching burgeoning leaders.

**ANTHONY KIM & ALEXIS GONZALES-BLACK**

Designed to foster flexibility and continuous innovation, this resource expands cutting-edge management and organizational techniques to empower schools with the agility and responsiveness vital to their new environment.

To order your copies, visit **corwin.com/leadership**

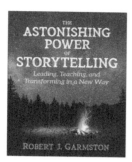

**ROBERT J. GARMSTON**

Stories have unique power to captivate and motivate action. This guidebook shows how to leverage storytelling to engage students.

**JOYCE L. EPSTEIN**

Strengthen programs of family and community engagement to promote equity and increase student success!

**DEAN T. SPAULDING & GAIL M. SMITH**

Help teams navigate the world of data analysis for ongoing school improvement with an easy-to-follow framework that dives deep into data-driven instruction.

**KENNETH LEITHWOOD**

By drawing on the numerous cases and stories, educators will gain a deep understanding of how to prepare the next wave of talented school leaders for success.

**ANGELINE A. ANDERSON, SUSAN K. BORG, & STEPHANIE L. EDGAR**

Centered on teacher voice and grounded in foundations of collaboration and data-informed planning, Transform Academy comes to life through its stories, and accompanying action steps.

**AMY TEPPER & PATRICK FLYNN**

Leaders know that feedback is essential to teacher development. This how-to guide helps leaders conduct comprehensive observations, analyze lessons, develop high-leverage action steps, and craft effective feedback.

**MICHAEL FULLAN, JOANNE QUINN, & JOANNE MCEACHEN**

This book defines what deep learning is, and takes up the question of how to mobilize complex whole-system change.

**JOANNE QUINN, JOANNE MCEACHEN, MICHAEL FULLAN, MAG GARDNER, & MAX DRUMMY**

This resource shows you how to design deep learning, measure progress, and assess the conditions to sustain innovation and mobilization.